The Path to Family Literacy

Building a comprehensive program, step by step

— Revised Edition —

By Carol Gabler and Jan Goethel

**With acknowledgment of input from all
partners and staff involved in the family literacy effort**

Proceeds from this project will be used to enhance
literacy efforts in the Chippewa Valley area.

D1473256

About the Authors

Carol Gabler is hired by Chippewa Valley Technical College to serve as Executive Director of Literacy Volunteers of America-Chippewa Valley in Eau Claire, Wisconsin. She is also a consultant for National LVA. She holds a bachelor's degree from the University of Minnesota and a master's degree from the University of Wisconsin-Eau Claire. She is a certified elementary education teacher, an Adult Basic Education instructor, and a reading specialist.

As a literacy consultant for Wisconsin, Ms. Gabler works with LVA affiliates statewide and acts in a consulting capacity for establishing family literacy programs. She serves on the Wisconsin Literacy Advisory Council and has been instrumental in developing partnerships between volunteer organizations and educational institutions.

At the national level Ms. Gabler serves in an advisory capacity to LVA, Inc. In 1993 she chaired the first LVA Family Literacy Institute in Louisville, Kentucky. She has been a presenter at the National Family Literacy Conferences sponsored by the National Center for Family Literacy.

Jan Goethel is currently working independently as a writer and also teaching in Education Outreach through the University of Wisconsin-Eau Claire. She is involved in LVA-Chippewa Valley both as a technical writer and as a tutor. Ms. Goethel has a bachelor's degree from the University of Wisconsin-Eau Claire and is a published author. She has been a presenter at the National Family Literacy Conference sponsored by the National Center for Family Literacy.

Copyright © 1996
Steck-Vaughn, in cooperation with National Center for Family Literacy
and Literacy Volunteers of America-Chippewa Valley
400 Eau Claire Street
Eau Claire, Wisconsin 54701

ISBN 0-8114-9249-4
Printed in the United States of America

Acknowledgments

Many dedicated and talented people have contributed to this effort.

The authors would like to recognize the following LVA-CV Family Literacy staff members, regular staff members, and Family Literacy Advisory Committee members for their valuable input:

Linda Bolgren	Michelle Livingston	Nikki Revak
Kathy Brunstad	Karol Machmeier	Rick Savolainen
Margaret Ann Bundy	Ellen Milne	Becky Shanley
Carolyn Carlson	Jane Morgan	Joanne Tews
Lynette Erickson	Jack O'Connell	Jane Wagner
Jan Happe	Terry Otto	Bette Wahl
Betsy Kell	Karen Peters	

Also the Lowes Creek Integrated Learning Center instructional and support staff

Our special thanks go to the following people for their insight and encouragement:

Caroline Beverstock	National LVA Board Member and literacy consultant
Anabel Newman	Past President, National Literacy Coalition

to the following people for their editing:

Dr. Martha Worthington	Professor emerita, University of Wisconsin-Eau Claire
Dr. Wilma Clark	Professor, University of Wisconsin-Eau Claire

and to the following people for data collection:

Dr. John Whooley	Professor emeritus, University of Wisconsin-Eau Claire
Wayne Atkins	President, LVA-CV Board of Directors

We would like to acknowledge the following reviewers:

Susan Paull	National Center for Family Literacy
Jan Cudahee	Literacy consultant, New York
Anita Findlen	Literacy consultant, Maine
Monica Notaro	Wisconsin Department of Public Instruction
Myrna Toney	Wisconsin Department of Public Instruction
Mary Anne Jackson	Wisconsin Technical College System
Susan Weinbeck	Family Literacy practitioner
Rachelle Otto	Family Literacy practitioner
Debra Schmid	Family Literacy practitioner
Phyllis Fabiny	LVA-CV Board of Directors
Linda Larkin	LVA-CV Board of Directors
Sandy Robbers	Indianhead Federated Library System
Eileen Emberson	Chippewa Valley Technical College

and the following technical assistants:

Michelle Allen	Chippewa Valley Technical College
Jackie Giles	Eau Claire Leader Telegram
Randy Krass	Documation technician
Stacy King	Documation typesetter

Preface

The following manual is intended as an aid for facilitators wanting to explain, implement, or expand a family literacy program. The authors have based their recommendations on sound research and on the experience of developing and successfully implementing the model program established by Literacy Volunteers of America-Chippewa Valley (LVA-CV) in Eau Claire, Wisconsin. This family literacy program was the first program to be validated nationally by the National Center for Family Literacy and the National Diffusion Network. In 1994 LVA-CV was recognized as Affiliate of the Year by the national organization of Literacy Volunteers of America.

The family literacy team in Eau Claire is an advocate of the "strengths" approach for all family literacy participants. This approach regards the family as a learning unit and builds upon the relationship between generations. The goal is to empower the parents to improve their own lives through literacy training, while giving their children a more vigorous start in school. This training should (1) be applicable to their daily lives and (2) reinforce existing skills and strengths. Parents who are convinced of the usefulness of knowledge are more likely to motivate and teach their own children (Ponzetti & Bodine, 1993).

The needs of this intergenerational target group are complex. These needs can best be met through a team approach, which draws input from many different areas of experience and expertise. Family literacy is most effective when all the issues can be addressed: adult basic education, employability, childcare needs of parents returning to school, school readiness skills for children, and other parenting concerns. When family support services are included, the parent is more able to concentrate on learning the skills needed to enhance economic self-sufficiency (Edlund, 1992; Nickse, 1990). The addition of community partners to the team enables more family support services to be offered. The Eau Claire program further enhances this effort with well-trained and fully-supported volunteers.

In the Eau Claire program, the initial family literacy effort involved story-hour sessions for children and parents together. Participating parents were enrolled in literacy training, primarily one-to-one tutoring. According to Nickse's 1990 classification of family programs by type of intervention (direct or indirect), this arrangement provided direct service to both the adult and the child. The training program used as the basis for this beginning program was *Reading With Children* (LVA, 1989).

As funding was secured, the program was expanded to include Adult Basic Education instruction, certified preschools, licensed childcare, transportation, and social services. This expansion enabled the program to supply the four basic components of comprehensive family literacy:

1. Education for the adult
2. Education for the preschooler
3. Parent education
4. Parent-child interaction activities

According to the National Center for Family Literacy, these four components, together with enough time and intensity of activity, are what truly constitute family literacy. The collaboration among these clearly defined approaches distinguishes family literacy from other intergenerational literacy efforts (Brizius & Foster, 1993).

Whatever the particular combination of services, positive impact upon the entire family demands that family literacy programs strengthen the connection between parent and child. These programs share a common understanding: the literacy development of children benefits from parents or caregivers who are also interested and involved in advancing their own literacy (Nuckolls, 1991).

If we are to achieve Goal #5 of the National Goals for Education —"By the year 2000, every adult American will be literate and will possess the knowledge and skills necessary to compete in a global economy and exercise the rights and responsibilities of citizenship" (U.S. Department of Education, 1990) — then it is all the more urgent that we reach children as effectively as possible.

Just as "there is no one right way to teach literacy to an adult new reader — no one approach or program so superior that all other approaches should be abandoned" (Newman & Beverstock, 1990, viii) — there is no perfect approach to family literacy. We must welcome many and varied solutions to the problems. Comprehensive family literacy, by its very nature, invites such integration.

The Path to Family Literacy
Table of Contents

Are you trying to explain or develop a

FAMILY LITERACY PROGRAM

but finding that

the pieces don't always fit together?

Well, you need not feel marooned.

We are here to help.

This manual will assist you in: 1. explaining the basic concepts
2. conducting the essential activities
3. implementing the key components
4. organizing a program
5. measuring progress

Information in this manual is based on the comprehensive model established by
Literacy Volunteers of America-Chippewa Valley in Eau Claire, Wisconsin.

The Eau Claire model is a grassroots endeavor that began with high hopes and a shoestring budget and has grown into a successful comprehensive family literacy program. By showing **YOU** what has worked for **US**, we may save you time and energy and perhaps spare you some frustration as well. Join us as we build a family literacy program, step by step . . . Join us on the path to literacy.

The basic concepts:

What is family literacy?
What are our goals?
Why build a comprehensive program?
Who are the partners?
How do we recruit them?
What do the partners provide?

Facilitators:

Watch for this poster image throughout the manual. It will suggest steps to take when building your own family literacy program. Think about how your program relates to the model being discussed.

What is family literacy?

An old idea, being revived . . .

The relevance of family to education is not a new concept. Recognition of family influence goes way back to the eighteenth century, as evidenced in pamphlets offering childrearing advice, through numerous movements in the 1920s and 1930s, to today's many diverse family education programs.

An attack on poverty, at its base level . . .

Today's focus on the family represents an increased awareness of the relationship between educational success and economic level. When a nation has nearly one in four young children living in poverty, with the highest rate found among minority children under six years old (National Center for Children in Poverty, 1990), there exists a large population facing greater risk of health impairment and educational disabilities. Family education programs are seen as a way to assist families, particularly poor families, in meeting their children's developmental needs.

A source of motivation . . .

Recent studies confirm that early childhood and school programs may be more successful when other family members are involved (Nuckolls, 1991). Characteristics of the family and home environment play a significant role in child development. When a home includes daily parent/child conversation, encouragement of reading, and interest in and a support for educational growth, the child evidences higher achievement (Walberg & Marjoribanks, 1976).

A means to improved attitudes . . .

Other research has shown that parental education is one of the best predictors of a child's school success (Wagner & Spratt, 1988). If the parents themselves are given the opportunity to further their education, they become better trained and more able to adapt to a rapidly changing technological environment. When parents feel competent in acquiring new skills, they gain confidence in teaching their own children. Education is then perceived as a lifelong pursuit, rather than a short-term challenge, and it becomes valuable. This attitude transfers to the children.

A team effort . . .

At its basic level, family literacy means the parent and child are learning together and enhancing both their lives. Family literacy programs consider parents and their children as a learning unit, assuming that they may profit from literacy as a shared experience (Nickse, 1989).

Specific definitions of family literacy vary, but for the purposes of this manual, we will be building a comprehensive program around the following basic components:

1. **Education for the adult**
   (Basic skills instruction for parents or primary caregivers)
2. **Education for the preschool child**
   (Developmental experiences for the young children)
3. **Parent education**
   (Assistance in parenting, employability, and personal growth areas)
4. **Parent-child interaction**
   (Opportunities for parents and children to learn together)

The fulfillment and integration of these basic components require teamwork. The family, the volunteers, and the teachers work as a team in pursuit of education. Together, they set joint goals that are attainable and appropriate for each specific situation. This ensures a more positive educational and recreational experience.

A comprehensive program expands the team with a network of school, government, volunteer, and community agencies. This collaboration helps parents overcome obstacles that lack of education and poverty have thrown in their path.

13

What are our goals in family literacy?

Our primary goal is to strengthen the family. Defined in terms of the basic components, we have the following:

For the adults:

to provide education relevant to their lives

This involves:

1. **Access to instruction in basic literacy skills.**

   Basic skills provide the tools for parents to improve themselves academically and ensure their ability to participate in literacy activities with their children.

2. **Readiness training for employment.**

   Career counseling and improved job skills prepare parents for greater success in their provider roles. We strive to reinforce existing skills and strengths.

For the children:

to provide developmental experiences conducive to continuing success in education

This involves:

1. **Stimulating opportunities for learning.**

   A classroom rich in sensory stimulation and geared to the developmental level of its students promotes academic and physical potential.

2. **A safe, supportive environment.**

   Acceptance of each child at his or her own level generates positive self-esteem in the child and fosters positive feelings toward learning. The classroom also provides an opportunity to develop social skills.

3. **Meaningful language experience.**

   Meaningful communication promotes the natural development of vocabulary in both verbal and written interaction.

For parent education:

> to provide assistance in developing the behavior patterns and skills necessary to function effectively as parents and providers

This involves:

1. **Education in child development.**
   When parents know what to expect from their children at certain stages and are shown alternative methods of behavior management, they are better equipped to deal with behavior problems.

2. **Support systems for positive personal growth.**
   This involves peer group activity as well as assistance from teachers and counselors and access to outside agencies.

3. **Good health and safety habits within the family.**
   Parents must recognize the significance of a healthy home environment.

4. **Preparation for employment.**
   Knowing what employers look for in job candidates can help parents find success in the job search.

For parent-child interaction:

> to provide opportunities for parents and their children to learn together

This involves:

1. **Staff and volunteers as role models.**
   As parents watch how teachers work with their children—in the classroom and during home visits—they become more comfortable in their own role as their child's first and most important teacher.

2. **Active participation in the education process.**
   The more ways we involve parents in the early education of their children, the more comfortable they will feel with the process in later years.

15

Why build a comprehensive program?

Many wonderful family literacy efforts, such as story hours and special parent-child interaction times, provide the beginning pieces for a comprehensive model. When the adult and the child both receive direct instruction (Nickse, 1990), the family benefits from the intense programming. Guided interaction between adult and child reinforces this approach. Thus the program strengthens literacy skills and family relationships at the same time. With the many different skills adults need to be functionally literate in an ever-changing world, a comprehensive program provides an excellent opportunity to prepare for the future.

But let's take a realistic look at the challenges we face:

> the needs that stand in the way of success in education
> for the population being considered

The pathway to improved literacy for an undereducated adult is one full of obstacles. The parent's ability to concentrate on learning is hindered by the struggle to make ends meet.

> the organizational task of pulling all the resources together
> to meet these needs

Community partners aren't just a good idea, they are a **necessity**, as the program is often too complicated and too expensive to be implemented by one service provider alone.

By drawing upon the varied programs and resources within a community, ways can be found to support and empower families. A comprehensive program draws these community resources in as partners in a team effort, without duplication of services.

With effective leadership and competent team players, a community can pool its resources and accomplish much more than individual agencies could.

A collaboration of partners can meet these needs through:
- Team effort
- Multi-dimensional services
- Shared vision
- Technological opportunities
- Creative financing
- Wider area of influence

Before you begin, you will need to know:
- **the needs of your target population**
- **the resources available in your community**
- **the services already being provided**

Don't be discouraged!
It's a hefty challenge,
but it can be met.

We are setting ourselves and the
participants up for failure
if we think we can solve
all their problems . . .
or if we think an integrated
program happens quickly . . .

But if we build a program carefully,
one piece at a time,
there will be progress
and everyone will benefit.

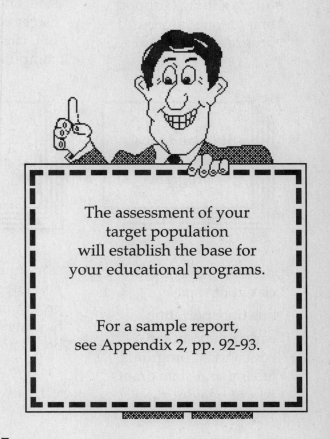

The assessment of your
target population
will establish the base for
your educational programs.

For a sample report,
see Appendix 2, pp. 92-93.

Who are the partners?

It takes a comprehensive program to deal with a complex situation.
The partners in family literacy work together to help overcome the obstacles.

Some potential partners are shown here as  HELP CARDS with suggestions of available services.

Literacy providers

* administration of project
* grant procurement
* tutor training/support
* one-on-one tutoring
* program evaluation

Vocational/ technical systems and universities

* Adult Basic Education instructors & curriculum
* state and federal funding
* career counseling
* ESL classes
* computer literacy

Childcare providers for siblings

may be found in:
* YMCAs
* churches
* volunteer groups

State and local educational programs

* preschool programs
* classroom space
* bus transportation
* early intervention educational programs
* federal and state grants
* parenting education

Libraries

* story hours
* possible space for literacy programming
* funding and donations
* books and other materials

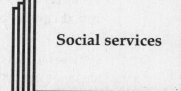

Social services

* JOBS program
* funding for childcare
* transportation funding
* student referrals
* monitoring parent progress

How do we recruit them?

The recruitment of partners is like a business venture. When you approach your community agencies as potential partners, be prepared to demonstrate how they also might benefit from this joint effort. Take the example of a JOBS program where recipients of aid must be in class 12-15 hours per week in order to qualify. Family literacy will meet this need while JOBS provides funding for childcare. Integrating services may be a more cost-effective solution for all.

If you are thinking of expanding your existing effort, build on the success you have already achieved. Take explanatory brochures along to educate potential partners about the program. (See Appendix 2, p. 98.) Consider taking a satisfied parent to visit a potential partner or sharing letters from former participants. Everyone likes to be part of a success story.

Make a list of the possible partners in your community. Be prepared with documentation of your community's needs.

Be creative.
Be persuasive.
Be persistent.

It is important to let partners know that you value their involvement. Recognition of their efforts can be accomplished through little things, such as including their logos on your pamphlets and stationery and mentioning them in press releases. (See Appendix 2, p. 98-114.) When representatives serve on your advisory committee, they become even more active. This also creates a more balanced governing body.

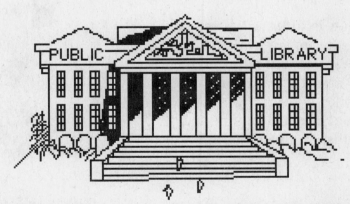

The primary role of the partners in a comprehensive family literacy program, of course, is to provide the positive components needed for success in learning. This cooperative effort tries to provide a seamless mesh of services that meet the students' needs. The partners are the ones who make things happen, functioning as both benefactors and facilitators. You can't accomplish such complex miracles without them!

What do the partners provide?

Partners collaborate to provide solutions for problems. Let's suppose we have assembled a group of parents interested in improving their skills. All are qualified to participate in a family literacy program. Let's suppose, also, that we have asked them about the problems they face in returning to school or pursuing a related goal.

We will use these hypothetical problems to illustrate the problem-and-solution aspect of family literacy opportunities. These problems are obstacles to learning, and facilitators of family literacy will discover that finding solutions is part of the daily routine. Some of these problems and solutions are illustrated below.

Obstacle: Reading and spelling are so hard for me that I have trouble in all subjects. I'm not sure I'm ready for school.

> **Solution**:
> Literacy providers specifically train tutors to help you develop these skills.

One-on-one tutoring is often a first step back to education. Tutors are available to assist students prior to enrollment in family literacy and after they are enrolled. Tutors usually make a commitment to work with individual parents for a period of at least six months. Tutoring is highly individualized.

Sometimes tutors and students work right in the public library or another public building. Sometimes they work in the family literacy site under the direction of the adult instructor.

Obstacle: I'd really like to be able to drive so my children and I aren't so isolated.

> **Solution**:
> As an adult, you are in charge of your own learning. Getting a driver's license is a good first goal for a beginning family literacy participant. The instructor and tutors can help you prepare for the written test.

Obstacle: I dropped out of high school. I can't get a decent job without a diploma.

> **Solution**:
> An instructor in family literacy will determine your current educational needs, help you set goals, and guide you in achieving them. Many students are working to pass their General Educational Development tests (GEDs). Others are upgrading skills needed for particular trades.

Instructors might be affiliated with vocational/technical college systems. Sometimes they are part of a community education program. Either way, they work closely with parents to develop educational plans suited to each parent's needs. They provide positive support — as well as a variety of learning opportunities, including cooperative learning and instruction in computer skills.

Obstacle: Sometimes I'm so upset by problems at home that I can't concentrate on school or assigned work.

Solution:
A family literacy program can link you with the services of a social worker to help you recognize and use your own support system. The social worker is available for crisis intervention as well, taking personal problems out of the class-room. Some programs are able to employ their own social worker part-time.

Obstacle: I still have a baby at home. I can't afford childcare. How can I possibly go back to school?

Solution:
Parents who qualify may obtain free childcare for siblings during class times.

Licensed daycare is available through a number of sources. As long as parents meet mandatory requirements, the JOBS program through social services agencies will pay for sibling childcare for children two years old and older. In other cases, the funds could come from an Even Start grant. Some programs have volunteers on-site providing childcare. In others, the parents start a childcare co-op among themselves.

Obstacle: I'm not sure what kind of work I can do, even if I meet my educational goal.

Solution:
Adult Basic Education instructors will assist you with career planning. They will help you assess your skills and interests as you seek to establish your own goals.

During jobs-exploration classes, speakers and career counselors will come in to assist in planning for the future. Communities have a wealth of individuals willing to share their expertise.

Obstacle: I am embarrassed by my lack of ability. School was always painful for me, so it is very hard to come back, and it is hard to pass on a positive attitude to my child.

Solution:
The parents in the adult class give support to each other, discuss problems, and share solutions. The scheduled parent-child activity times in your child's classroom will help you feel more at ease in a learning situation. As you feel better about school, this attitude will be passed on to your child.

Parents who have been in this program praise the camaraderie within the group.

Obstacle: I have no car. How do we get to school?

Solution:
Busing of parents and children might be arranged through the public schools. Transportation funding is also available for qualified participants through JOBS, Head Start, and Even Start. Sometimes parents carpool together.
Many ride city buses.

Creative problem solving is required to help parents who have several young children coordinate their schedules with the children's schedules. In an ideal family literacy setting, the adult classroom is located in the same building that provides a Head Start, kindergarten or preschool program as well as sibling childcare. When this is not possible, each family's needs will have to be met individually.

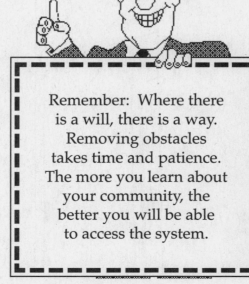

Remember: Where there is a will, there is a way. Removing obstacles takes time and patience. The more you learn about your community, the better you will be able to access the system.

Obstacle: I don't know how to help my child get ready for kindergarten.

Solution:
Through the family literacy program, your child will attend preschool classes to learn age-appropriate skills. A parenting instructor will also show you ways to help your child prepare for school.

Trained and certified preschool teachers provide developmental experiences. The emphasis is on developing the child's ability:

> to grasp reading readiness skills
> to make choices and decisions
> to work with other children and adults cooperatively
> to use self-discipline in completing tasks
> to communicate thoughts, ideas and feelings
> to express himself/herself creatively

When parents are involved in their children's classroom activities, they gain skill and confidence in their role as the child's primary teacher.

Obstacle: My parents were not very good role models when I was growing up. I want to be a better parent to my own children, but I don't know how.

> **Solution:**
> Parenting classes are required in the family literacy program. The instructor meets with the parents regularly and schedules supervised parent-child interaction time.

Parent education is based on shared experience. Its basic goals are to:

1. teach parents how to be teachers to their own children
2. help parents understand child development: physical, cognitive, social, and emotional
3. model positive alternatives for guiding child behavior
4. facilitate school readiness and school success
5. improve parental attitude toward education
6. teach good health, nutrition, and safety habits
7. deal with family issues (stress, abuse, single parenthood, relationships, etc.)
8. help parents develop the skills and behavior patterns essential to successful employment
9. provide information about community resources

The essential activities:

How important is publicity?
Who recruits the families?
Who can participate?

How do these concepts apply to
English as a Second Language programs?

How can volunteers help?

Every intergenerational
literacy program will have
its own unique needs.
You must assess your
target population,
identify your needs,
then mold your approach
and materials
to address those needs.

How important is publicity?

Publicity is an essential part of any strong program. By letting the community know what you are doing, you can lure public support as well as prospective participants. Parents wishing to return to school will know whom to contact. Prospective partners will be aware of the positive image the program presents to the community. Contributors will recognize the signs of diligent effort. Potential volunteers will be impressed by a well-organized effort.

There are a number of places to scout out experienced and talented individuals to assist you with publicity. One would be the local college or university, if you have one nearby. The English department or journalism department may be able to direct you to a student needing an internship or special project.

If you don't have a university or college nearby, perhaps a local print shop, newspaper, or professional organization could suggest a willing volunteer.

Do you have a partner who will help promote the program? Designate someone to handle publicity.

See Appendix 2, p. 98, for sample brochures and flyers.

It will help if you can get a volunteer with knowledge in technical writing, because it takes a lot of time to develop meaningful flyers and brochures for distribution to parents, partners, and funders.

The more professional-looking your press releases and brochures are, the more impressive they will be.

Remember: it will take repeated exposure for potential families, partners, and funders to really understand what you are trying to accomplish.

We have found that if we recognize our volunteers, respect their time constraints, and work around their schedules, everyone wins and feels good about participating. Each week we place a Stars in Literacy ad on the local television station and in the newspaper, honoring a different individual or group. We feature parents, partners, volunteers, and staffers in this recognition. Both newspaper space and air time are donations.

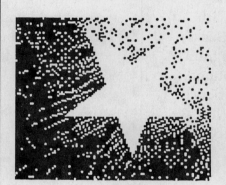

LVA
Stars in
Literacy

"Reading is a wonderful way to share time with your child. My friends Jackie and Katie love to read about me, King Babar. Celebrate International Literacy Day today by reading a book to your child."

King Babar
(Gary Giles - Arby's Restaurant)

If you or someone you know would like more information about available help, call 834-0222.

Leader-Telegram

WQOW•TV 18
Eau Claire

LITERACY VOLUNTEERS of AMERICA Inc.
834-0222

Who recruits the families?

A push in the right direction may come from numerous sources:

1. **Social services/human services agencies**
   The **JOBS** program (Job Opportunity and Basic Skills) is a state and federal work program for **AFDC** (Aid to Families with Dependent Children) recipients. **JOBS** is a strong partner in a family literacy program because participants are required to attend classes and/or complete a work experience to receive financial assistance. **JTPA** (Job Training Partnership Act) is another federal program that might be a source for participants.

   > List the agencies that could help you recruit. List your rules of eligibility. These two factors are interrelated.
   >
   > Agencies often use brochures to recruit parents.

2. **Schools**
   Early childhood educational programs, such as Head Start and Early Childhood Exceptional Educational Needs, are a possible source of participants. In the public school system, close cooperation with Chapter 1 or Chapter 2 programs can be a great asset.

3. **Vocational/technical colleges and community education programs**
   Instructors often encounter students with young children who could benefit from a family literacy program.

4. **Literacy programs**
   Staff members in agencies such as literacy programs and libraries are aware of families in need of assistance.

5. **Employers**
   Many companies support literacy training.

6. **Local public housing authority and homeless shelters**

7. **Self-referral**
   Often friends tell friends about the program.
   Flyers can be posted in churches, housing projects, gas stations, social service agencies, grocery stores, and at kindergarten registration.

Who can participate?

Clear rules for eligibility help a program function smoothly.

Criteria for a comprehensive family literacy program might look like this, depending on participants' needs, funding, and different agency requirements:

1. Parents must have children eligible for preschool.

2. Parents must be eighteen (18) years of age or older.

3. Parents must need help in literacy skills to function successfully in the community.

4. Parents and children must commit to attend together regularly.

5. Parents seeking financial assistance through social services must meet requirements of the JOBS program or JTPA (see previous page).

6. Children must reside in a Chapter 1 school attendance area to qualify for **Even Start** programming. Parents must also meet specific requirements.

   (Chapter 1 is federal funding distributed through state departments of public instruction to meet special needs. The Even Start program is federal funding designed to integrate early childhood education with adult education to improve educational opportunities for adults and children between birth and 8. See Appendix 2, p. 96, for more information.)

What is involved in registering parents?

Families are identified through sources such as those listed on page 30. The facilitator might start in the spring by including interest letters in the application packets for Head Start and other similar programs. Parents who respond could be sent a letter during the summer. (See the sample in Appendix 2, p. 118.) In July JOBS case managers, other social workers, and public school employees are contacted to remind them to submit by mid-August the names of the people they want enrolled. In late August there are opportunities to attend Head Start orientation meetings to talk about the program.

Once a potential family is identified, the parent is contacted personally by a staff member. An interview is arranged, either in the parent's home or in a public location. The initial interview is informal, with the facilitator explaining the program to the parent. Conversation with the parent will reveal the obvious needs that must be met in that particular family for the parent to return to school.

Ideally, everyone should be ready to start at the same time. In reality, recruitment is an ongoing process. Families move, drop out, get their high school equivalency diplomas, and so forth, so referrals from most sources continue to come in throughout the year. When the referral is received, the facilitator attempts to place the child and parent as soon as possible. Operating on a semester basis makes it a little easier to control movement in and out of the program. Many programs offer fall, winter, and summer sessions.

According to a statement prepared by the International Reading Association Family Literacy Commission, "successful family literacy programs respect and understand the diversity of the families they serve. They build upon literacy behaviors already present in families. . . . Successful family literacy programs do not try to 'correct' or 'fix' the family. Rather, they view intervention as a supplement to the interactions that already exist." (International Reading Association, 1994)

"Shifting gears from thinking that these are families with problems to opening our eyes to see resources and strengths is one way staff can aid families in acknowledging their own strengths." (PLUS report, 1993, p. 13.)

It is important to know the needs and characteristics of your target population. For tips on assessing these needs, see Appendix 2, page 92.

See guidelines for selection of participants on page 97.

How can a facilitator increase retention in a program?

Retention of participants can be challenging. Consider the following suggestions:

1. Maintain flexibility in programming.
   - Arrange classes to fit family schedules and public school calendars.
   - Adjust to meet work and class requirements of other programs.

2. Emphasize direct benefits for parents and clearly articulate your expectations.
   - Stress improved education and employment opportunities.
   - Explain how these goals can be attained.

3. Be responsive to families' multiple needs.
   - Help meet sibling childcare and transportation needs.
   - Help parents set realistic goals, with some easily achieved objectives.
   - Recognize that timing is not always going to be right; allow for comfortable re-entry into the program.

4. Provide incentives and tangible rewards for participation. (YMCA memberships, free childcare, free books, T-shirts, etc.)

5. Provide a nonthreatening, "user friendly" classroom environment.
   - Build in opportunities for parents and children to experience success.

6. Present a well-organized program.
   - Follow sound educational practices appropriate for your participants.
   - Schedule time for staff and partners to interact and plan.

7. Schedule regular, prearranged home visits.
   - Build upon literacy behaviors already present in families, using materials and approaches tailored to each individual family.
   - Give parents an active role in determining the content of these visits.
   - Use this as an opportunity to pay special attention to the needs and interests of the parent, and to share information about other community resources.

The challenges to implementing home visits:
- Home visits require staff trained to deal with potential issues such as abuse, violence, substance abuse, safety, and emergency procedures.
- Sometimes the home is not a safe place, or the family prefers that no one come to the home. Then an alternative meeting place must be arranged.
- Sensitivity to family cultures and native language is essential.

How do these concepts apply to
English as a Second Language programs?

The challenge of teaching basic skills when English is not the primary language spoken in the home is one that draws upon the creativity and resourcefulness of a family literacy staff. The family should be viewed as an especially valuable resource in this situation, for it is intrinsic to the support system of both the adult and the child.

Building upon family strengths may be the most productive approach. As Ranard (1989) points out, "an approach that views the family — both adults and children — as a combined resource for learning is particularly well suited to the cultural backgrounds and social circumstances of refugee families [who see] the family rather than the individual as the basic unit of society" (p. 1).

There are other factors crucial to a successful ESL family literacy program:

Collaboration with the ethnic community leaders and its adult members
These individuals should be involved in each step of program planning and implementation. This ensures support for the endeavor from those in a position to affect the program. It also increases awareness and broadens understanding on the part of the literacy provider.

Cooperation with other agencies who work with this language group
Sharing ideas and resources with ESL programs in the community (e.g., universities, technical colleges or public school systems) helps broaden knowledge and meet other needs, such as for interpreters and other bilingual support.

Appreciation of traditional cultures
"Children who understand their own background and culture are more likely to have the self-esteem needed to acquire a second language and culture. Adults whose knowledge and wisdom are valued are in a better position to support their children in school and elsewhere; they are also in a better position to be helped by their children without having their dignity or their role as parent threatened." (Weinstein-Shr, 1989)

Relevance of education to the life experiences of the participants
Incorporating natural language and culture into the educational environment will create a link with the new language. The most accessible knowledge is that which relates directly to our own experiences.

Helpful hints for ESL facilitators:

To achieve successful collaboration and planning
- have a strong leader on staff who is from the culture or speaks the language.
- conduct interviews and home visits in the family's first language, if possible.
- involve the parents in the planning process. They know best what they want and need.
- maintain open and honest dialogue with ethnic community leaders.

To provide an organized, effective program
- maintain contact with other community agencies.
- provide inservice for your ESL staff periodically. The problems encountered and approaches used within ESL programs differ from those typically found in classes for English-speaking adults.
- make use of materials specifically designed for ESL programs. (See the resource list in Appendix 4, p. 174.)

To incorporate cultural appreciation
- use volunteers from the native language community.
- learn as much as you can about other cultures.
- use literature from that culture or language base.

To maintain relevance in educational services offered
- use materials that relate to daily needs: children's books, utility bills, newspapers, etc.
- encourage parent-child interaction in the family's first language.
- use a natural, whole language approach, treating phonics and grammar as tools, not as ends in themselves.
- build on the interests and knowledge of the adult, rather than the instructor.
- make sure parenting materials are culturally sensitive and appropriate for the target group (not all from the white majority middle class perspective).
- incorporate "hands-on" verbal experiences that can later be translated into written language (example: cooking together, then writing down recipes).

> **Every intergenerational literacy program will have its own unique needs -- whether these be in the area of teaching English as a second language or elsewhere. The most important thing is to identify your program needs, then adapt or create materials that address those particular concerns.**

How can volunteers help?

Volunteers are an integral part of our family literacy program. They serve as tutors in adult education, assistants in preschool and childcare, and role models for parent-child interaction activities. Even our Board of Directors gets involved through strategic planning, fund raising, public relations, and running the RIF program.

The volunteers with the greatest impact on adult learning are the tutors, the people who provide one-to-one instruction for the parents in the program.

> "Attendance is more regular when students know their tutor will be there to help."
>
> (K. Brunstad, ABE instructor)

Where can we get tutors?

Your source of tutors will depend on which major organization is behind your comprehensive literacy effort. In our case, the coordinating agency is Literacy Volunteers of America.

Any literacy provider would most likely welcome the opportunity to provide trained tutors to support your effort. You will have to work together to mesh your programs, so that it is a successful experience for everyone.

If your community does not have an organization that promotes literacy, contact an organization of retired teachers or your local reading council for suggestions. You might also contact the agencies listed on pages 165-167. Many of these can provide the materials and information needed to begin your own tutor training program.

What about training for tutors?

The methods used should be based on sound educational research as well as practice in the field. In our program an experienced trainer conducts 14-16 hours of workshops that prepare volunteers to work with adult students.

The topics covered include:
    characteristics of an adult learner
    different approaches used with adults
    preparation of lesson plans
    familiarity with materials adults use
        when upgrading their skills

The tutor trainer also provides the much-needed tutor support that ensures a successful experience when working with a student.

Our policy of 50/50 management (50 percent of time spent on training, 50 percent spent on supporting tutor and student) has increased our success in retention of volunteer tutors.
(See next page for more detail.)

Tips for tutors

Relationships between tutors and students take time and patience to develop. It is important to build trust and rapport.

Student absenteeism can be frustrating. The instructor and literacy provider will work with you to find a solution if this is a continuing problem.

Progress may seem slow. Be patient, and take things one step at a time. Both you and the student need to set realistic goals.

Students may share personal problems with you. This is normal. However, you are not expected to solve them. Don't hesitate to discuss your concerns with the instructor or literacy provider staff. They are there to support you.

You are a role model for your student. In addition to academic assistance, you may find yourself teaching the skills needed to organize, study, and manage time effectively.

For a sample learning plan to be shared with a tutor, see Appendix 2, page 120.

A tutor may spend longer periods of time with a student than the instructor will. Ideally, a tutor should come in twice a week for 1 to 1 1/2 hours.

It is important to make tutors feel like a valuable part of the team.

(See the volunteer tutor job description for more detail — Appendix 1, p. 86.)

The **50/50 Program Management System** (DuPrey, 1992) is a training program for leaders in literacy efforts. It is based on the concept that all well-managed volunteer literacy programs, regardless of size, location, or educational approach, have something in common. They all seek to bring volunteers and learners into the program and then keep them involved. Balancing **50 percent intake** and **50 percent support** in funding and activities can assure the quality and length of tutor training and tutor retention. (*Education News*, 1994)

Implementing
the key components:

How do we educate the adults?
How do we educate the children?
What do we offer in parent education?
How do we facilitate parent-child interaction?

We have suggested ways
to recruit and retain families
in your
comprehensive program.

Now we will take a
closer look at the
four key components,
considering both their content
and the more personal side
of the program.

How do we educate the adults?

Our primary goal for adults is to provide education relevant to their lives.

There are two major areas of emphasis:

- **Basic skills instruction** provides the tools for parents to improve themselves academically and ensure their ability to participate in literacy activities with their children. Adult basic education (ABE) includes instruction in areas such as reading, writing, and mathematics. English as a Second Language (ESL) programs are available, as well as preparation for the general educational development (GED) tests.

- **Readiness training for employment** prepares parents for greater success in their provider roles. With guidance adults explore career interests and determine their existing strengths. They learn how to write resumes, find jobs, and keep jobs. The availability of computers is a definite asset, since computers are an integral part of the work world as well as a learning tool. (See page 48.)

Creating a learning environment that meets the needs of adult students is essential to a successful adult education program. In many states adults on welfare are required to return to work, so family literacy programs must offer flexibility and assistance in arranging parents' schedules to accommodate school, work, and the needs of their children.

The challenge is to create a nonthreatening atmosphere in which adults are expected to share in the responsibility for their learning.

A program is more likely to succeed when it:

1. tailors learning programs to individual students
2. values adults for their life experiences
3. recognizes individual differences and individual goals
4. involves adult students in selection of course content as well as evaluation of progress
5. offers material with an opportunity for immediate application
6. provides opportunity for work experience.

Designing an individualized learning program for each adult:

1. Interview the student to assess individual needs.
   You need to know the family situation, as well as academic background.

2. Make an assessment of the student's abilities.
   What your program can do will be influenced by your state's requirements for adult basic education. Our assessments, for example, are based on portfolios containing interview data, writing samples, standardized test scores, and background reports from referral agencies. Assessment will also determine which students need help learning how to study and prepare for tests.

3. Help the student set realistic short- and long-term goals.

Some examples of goals:
improve basic skills
acquire citizenship
pass the written driver's test
obtain a part-time job
pass a civil service exam
pass the GED tests
earn high school equivalency diploma
       (same as GED in most states, but not all)
upgrade skills to enter a training program

4. Develop an individualized instruction plan.
   This plan will include academic goals as well as parenting/personal development. (See Appendix 2, p. 120, for a sample learning plan.)

5. Maintain ongoing evaluation of the student's progress.
   Whereas standardized tests used to be the method of choice in measuring knowledge, now people in the area of evaluation are also using alternative methods of assessment. The alternative methods suggested by Holt (1994) are:
   1. Surveys
   2. Interviews
   3. Observation measures
   4. Performance samples

These evaluation procedures provide more immediate feedback for the planning staff. (See pages 67-71 for more information.)

What is a typical day like in our Adult Basic Education classroom?

9:00 AM	Announcements for the day
9:15 AM	Group activity. Examples: journal or essay writing, current events discussion, study skills instruction
9:45 AM*	Individualized ABE instruction. Example: GED preparation in math
10:25 AM	Break
10:40 AM	Parenting classes or parent and child interaction time
12:00-12:30 PM	Lunch
12:30 PM	Individualized ABE instruction. Example: GED preparation in literature and the arts
2:20 PM	Break
2:35 PM	Parenting/personal growth and employability classes
3:30 PM	Pick up children and talk to preschool teacher

* This is the time period when parents take turns assisting in the preschool classroom. The schedule may vary. (See a sample learning plan in Appendix 2, p. 120.)

From our experience:

The schedule set by the advisory committee must take many factors into consideration, such as the work hours required along with the educational hours for JOBS participants. Holding classes three days a week leaves Tuesdays and Thursdays available to meet this requirement. Students can also work during the summer.

Our annual calendar coordinates with area public schools and the technical college. The two 16-week semesters begin in late August and end in early May. This enables us to take advantage of busing, and parents can be home with older siblings when they are on vacation from school.

Summer library activities, YMCA classes, and city recreation programs are encouraged. LVA tutors are available for students who want to continue their studies.

It is important that families know what is expected of them when they enroll. Adults must be ready to make a commitment to the program and to accept responsibility for their own learning. See the attendance and behavior policy in Appendix 3, Form D.

Tips from an adult education instructor:

Be interested in your students!
Don't be afraid to ask adults about their prior school experiences. This will give you lots of good insight.

Be patient!
Most adults will readily admit to needing help in mathematics. It may take longer for them to ask for help in other areas.

Be upbeat!
Celebrate all the successes you can: someone passing one of the GED tests, a month of good attendance, someone getting a driver's license, etc.

Be consistent!
Adults respect teachers who maintain a sense of structure and a calm routine.

Be flexible!
Your students will experience daily highs and lows. Their progress will often be affected by trauma in their lives. Don't let the setbacks discourage you: there will lots of progress over the long term!

(K. Brunstad, ABE lead instructor)

How to use volunteers effectively:

Spend extra time getting ready for volunteers. It will really pay dividends! The more volunteers know about the program, the classroom set-up, the teacher's methods and philosophy, and their assigned students, the more they will enjoy the time and be able to help the teacher!

(See the job description for a volunteer tutor, p. 86)

What about students who drop out, then want to come back?

A careful intake procedure should help screen out participants who are not ready, but there are always unforeseen reasons why a student will find it necessary to drop out of the family literacy program. Examples might be a change in the home situation, transportation difficulties, language barrier, new family obligations, or significant relationships threatened by the student's success. The important thing when the student comes back is to determine what extra assistance is needed. Perhaps goals need to be clarified or redefined. Be positive. Be supportive. Appreciate the fact that it takes courage to come back . . .

How do we educate the children?

The goal of early childhood education is to provide developmental experiences conducive to continuing success in education.

This requires:
Stimulating opportunities for learning

A stimulating environment offers a variety of developmentally appropriate materials and a fully trained staff.

A safe, supportive environment

The physical environment meets the requirements for state licensing for childcare. The emotional environment generates positive self-esteem and healthy social interaction skills.

Meaningful language experience

Meaningful communication promotes the natural growth of language.

Creating an environment that meets the needs of young children:

According to a position statement issued by the National Association for the Education of Young Children, effective early childhood education must be developmentally appropriate. For children to fully understand and remember what they have learned, whether it is related to reading, mathematics, or other subject matter areas, the information must be meaningful to the child in context of the child's experience and development. (NAEYC, 1986)

Young children learn about the world around them through active exploration and interaction with objects and people. If information is relevant to their world, they will be motivated to learn and understand. Consequently we offer the following:

- Physical exercise that improves coordination, provides an appropriate outlet for energy, and bolsters the child's self-confidence

- Cognitive stimulation that meets a range of developmental needs

- Meaningful communication that promotes the natural development of language

- Activities and interactions that foster positive self-esteem and positive feelings toward learning

- Opportunities that strengthen social skills—such as cooperating, helping, negotiating, and solving interpersonal problems through dialog.

What is a typical day like in our preschool classroom?

The following is the approximate schedule of a half-day session:

8:45 AM	Arrival of buses
8:45-9:00 AM	Opening: informal conversation
9:00-9:40 AM	Breakfast/bathroom duties
9:40-10:05 AM	Story time: large group or individual book time
10:05-10:25 AM	Small group activity: such as art project or cognitive activity (color matching, counting, etc.)
10:25-11:10 AM	Work time: (High/ Scope* curriculum applied)
	— **plan** day's activity
	— **do** as planned
	Snack time/bathroom breaks as needed
11:10-11:20 AM	Clean-up
11:20-11:30 AM	Closing: **review** morning's activities
11:30 AM	Departure of buses

*Hohmann, Banet, & Weikart 1979

Other elements integrated into this pattern are outdoor playtime, large muscle activities, and scheduled weekly parent-child activities. Parents assisting in the classroom can be as involved as they want to be. The teachers strive to make this interaction positive and comfortable for both parents and children.

From our experience:

Like all other elements in a family literacy endeavor, the preschool program must be flexible, adapting to needs and facilities. Our program runs two different preschools. One is connected with the public schools and under the guidance of the Head Start program. The parents attend class in the same school building. The other class is located at the YMCA, with the parents attending class in a neighboring building. The curriculum used in the two programs is similar but varies according to the ages of the children. Children attending school at the YMCA have access to a gymnasium and swimming pool. The YMCA program runs for the full day, while Head Start is set up in two separate half-day sessions. Head Start children whose parents are in the family literacy program must be bused to the YMCA for the afternoon session. Although it is complicated, it works.

45

Tips for dealing with an at-risk population:

If you expect to be effective, you need to deal with the whole family and all of its potential domestic problems. This group is more challenging in that members of it often lack "normal" childhood experiences, such as pedaling a tricycle.

Be nurturing and patient. Begin at the level where children **are**, not where you feel they **should be**.

Every child has special needs, but every child has **unique talents**. Find that uniqueness — build on the child's strengths. Look for opportunities to bring that particular skill up to age level first, and the other areas will follow.

Always build on the positive.

(B. Shanley, preschool teacher)

Tips for effective use of volunteers:

Always treat your volunteers as if they were other professionals, whether they are adults from the community, college students needing experience, or parents of your students.

Make your volunteers feel welcome, important, and appreciated. Greet them. Introduce them to the class. Help them to feel comfortable in the classroom setting.

Encourage volunteers to interact in many different ways with the children. Whether they read to the children, do art or physical activities with them, or simply talk to them, the adults are showing that they care about what the children learn.

Volunteers feel satisfied if they have helped the program. Thank them!

(L. Erickson, preschool teacher)

What do we offer in parent education?

Our goal for parent education is to assist parents in developing the behavior patterns and skills necessary to function more effectively as parents and providers.

This component points right to the heart of family literacy programs — **the family**.

A healthy parent is essential to a healthy family. Consequently, parent education must provide a support system for personal growth. However, it is also important for parents to understand how their own actions shape the lives of their children in all major areas: health, safety, education, self-image, attitudes, values, and so on. When parents can share parenting concerns, guided by a trained and experienced facilitator, the new strategies they learn may benefit the whole family.

According to Ponzetti and Bodine (1993), the content of parent education includes at least three distinct elements:

1. **Parenting sessions**
2. **Parent support services**
3. **Parental involvement**

In our program we add a fourth element:

4. **Preparation for employment**

The course of study is strongly influenced by the results of surveys assessing the interests and needs of current participants. (See the sample surveys in the Forms section.)

These segments may be offered through many different public and private agencies and groups, or by a single facilitator. Although parent education is integrated into some adult basic education programs throughout the country, most programs of this nature are offered by early childhood programs or through community agencies, such as churches and schools (Landerholm, 1984). When these parent education components are coordinated directly with the efforts being made in child education and family welfare — treating the family as a unit — their relevance and applicability to family life is increased.

Integration of all four components occurs throughout the program. One of the most valuable vehicles for this integration is **home visiting**. Home visits bring literacy activities into the home, assist with transitions to other academic programs, create an opportunity to apply what has been learned in parenting sessions, and furnish role models for parent-child interactions.

Suggested units for <u>parenting sessions</u>:

1. **Child development**
   a. Factors that influence growth and development
   b. Areas of development and appropriate expectations
   c. Role of play in development
2. **Guiding children's behavior**
   a. Communicating positively
   b. Encouraging and building self-esteem
   c. Effective discipline
   d. Problem solving
3. **Learning and readiness**
   a. Encouraging readiness skills in reading, writing, etc.
   b. Understanding learning problems
   c. Being aware of the effect of television on families
   d. Developing a partnership with schools and teachers
4. **Healthy families**
   a. Traits of a healthy family
   b. Coping with stress and building positive relationships
   c. Dealing with abuse
   d. Using community resources
   e. Providing good health, nutrition and safety
5. **Parent-child interaction** (See pp. 50-52.)

(Machmeier, 1993)

Some methods that can be used in parenting education:
Large group discussions, small group activities
Role playing
Texts, handouts, videos, speakers, instructor presentations
Resources to check out for home use
Potluck suppers and picnics

Potential <u>parent support services</u>:

Parent support is the portion of parent education that attempts to deal with the practical realities of life within this particular population. Outside sources provide many of the available support services, such as transportation, childcare, counseling, referral for alcohol and drug addiction treatment, or assistance with legal, medical, or housing issues. However, there is also an element of peer support, in which the program participants are able to share problems and solutions with each other, under the guidance of the facilitator. These parenting concerns are often integrated into the class curriculum as well, when there is a common interest in specific topics.

Ways to encourage <u>parental involvement</u>:

Parent involvement focuses on engaging the parent in the child's formal educational process both in the home and at school.

Ways to get parents involved:
conferences with teachers
parent-child fieldtrips
home visits by the preschool teacher
volunteering in the children's room
parent-child "hands-on" activities
reading and writing activities for the
    parent and child
special holiday events in the classroom
story hours at libraries or schools
activities planned and led by parents
take-home activities from school
(See page 50 for more information.)

You may encounter parents who are not enthusiastic about being required to participate in the children's classroom or to attend parenting classes.

If their goals do not extend beyond adult education, your challenge will be to make them more aware of their roles as teachers.

Ways to help parents <u>prepare for employment</u>:

1. **Behavior patterns:** Provide activities that help parents
   a. build self-confidence and self-esteem.
   b. develop productive communication patterns.
   c. learn healthy ways to deal with stress.
   d. make a good impression in an interview.

2. **Skills:** Provide opportunities for parents to
   a. practice completing resumes and applications.
   b. acquire successful interview techniques.
   c. practice a work ethic which exhibits
      • punctuality
      • reliability
      • tact
      • respect for others
      • careful attention to instruction
   d. expand consumer awareness.
   e. improve money management.
   f. fulfill the requirements of sponsoring agencies (such as the JOBS program, which requires a resume and participation in a work experience).

How do we facilitate parent-child interaction?

Our goal in parent-child interaction is to provide opportunities for parents and their children to learn together.

Parents in the classroom setting can observe how the teacher and volunteers interact with the children. Home visits provide an opportunity for this, as well. The benefits are two-fold:

1. Observation of role models helps parents become more comfortable in their own role as their child's first and most important teacher.

2. Active participation in the education process helps parents develop a more positive attitude toward school in general.

In family literacy, the phrase **"PACT time"** stands for
Parent And Child Together time.

Regularly scheduled PACT time exposes parents to many educational activities and provides the opportunity to strengthen their relationship with their children. After each interaction, parents in our program write in their PACT journals, describing the experience and their personal reactions to it. (See the journal entry form in Appendix 3, Form V.) Parents periodically review this journal to evaluate their own progress. Through this evaluation they can detect changes in behavior, attitudes, and feelings—in themselves and in the children. They generally take this journal along when they have conferences with the parenting instructor.

Interaction can be achieved in a number of ways:

- **Regularly scheduled group activities**
  These may focus on specific themes, such as a teddy bear picnic or seasonal celebrations.

  Sometimes our parents and children take field trips to a farm, the museum, a park, and even a children's theater performance. Other times they might learn a new game in the gym or work on an art project together.

- **One-on-one activities designed for the classroom**
  This activity time may be closely structured, or it may be left open for the parent and child to choose what they want to do together. Parents are encouraged to read books to their children and to discuss what they read. This is a valuable experience for both, particularly when the parents have been given some assistance in skillful oral reading and effective interaction. Reading, talking, and listening all help strengthen whole language skills. These guided interactions also allow the teachers to observe and nurture communication in parent-child relationships.

- **One-on-one activities designed to be taken home**
  Our parenting instructor extends this healthy interaction to the home setting by assembling kits called **Parent Pacs.** These kits consist of canvas or plastic tote bags containing all the materials and instructions for a parent-and-child activity. A kit may be kept at home for one month. It may also be used during home visits.

  Parent Pacs contain different items for different activities:
  - One kit may contain a book and its corresponding audio tape.
  - Another may contain the basic story line and all the supplies for making a simple illustrated storybook.
  - A third may contain an erasable "magic slate" or stencils to encourage pre-writing activity.

  Parents are expected to write their reactions to each activity with the children in their interaction journals.

- **Informal performances for the parents**
  Children benefit from planning, practicing, and performing simple "shows" for their parents. One easy way to do this is to select a familiar story for the children to dramatize. Our classes have enjoyed doing "Goldilocks and the Three Bears."

  This activity will be more successful if you:
  - Allow the children to take an active role in planning the performance, such as choosing the props and deciding when to use them.
  - Have the teacher narrate and the children supply the dialog.
  - Prepare the parents to expect the unexpected. That way they will see each child as successful, whether they know all the lines, act out all the motions, or choose to be part of the audience.

- **Collaborative parent-child writing projects**
  Every year in our program we conduct our parents and children through progressive writing activities that prepare them to produce an illustrated story together. The parent writes the story as the child dictates, then the parent edits the tale and submits it with the child's drawing to be "published" in a book. A detailed outline of this project may be found in *Telling Tales*. (See page 172.)

- **Reading Is Fundamental (RIF) activities**

  RIF is a federal program which encourages reading and provides limited funding for qualified programs. Participating publishers offer a discount to programs which give books to children. (See page 172 for more information.)

  RIF programs at the elementary level often take place in schools. Preschool programs, such as ours, are readily adaptable to libraries, daycare, and volunteer organizations. In our program, the literacy board of directors takes on this task.

  Our RIF committee, composed of board members and other enthusiastic volunteers, presents three RIF events per year. Each has a theme, with corresponding activities, snacks, and free books. Parents attend with their children, ages 4 to 6. The parents are encouraged to join in the games and other activities. Teachers in our family literacy children's classrooms prepare the children for the event by reading the theme books to them ahead of time.

  One of our favorite RIF events had a farm theme, with visiting farm animals and a simplified version of country line-dancing. The featured book was *Big Red Barn*, by Margaret Wise Brown (Harper & Rowe, 1989).

How else can volunteers assist parent-child interaction?

Volunteers can provide additional role models for parents. They also fill in for a parent who is testing during interaction time. Sometimes a single parent with more than one child in the program needs the help of a volunteer to provide one-to-one contact with the children.

From one mother in our program: "My daughter benefited so much from the literacy program last year that she is now in Head Start. After seeing first hand what she does, the rewards are not measured in dollars and cents, but by the gleam in her eyes and the big smile on her face. Her first words every morning are, do we have school today?"

(V. De Ford, family literacy participant)

Organization:

Who governs the program?
Who coordinates the components?
Who pays for all this?

Your structure will likely
differ from ours.
It is important, however, to
have a designated coordinator
willing to take responsibility
for the program and a
governing body willing to
support, monitor and advise
the coordinator.

Who governs the program?

The governing body usually evolves when someone is willing to take responsibility and lead the way. Any partner could fill this role. Sometimes the largest funding source determines who will take charge.

Every program is different. In our case, major policy decisions are made by the governing body of Literacy Volunteers of America-Chippewa Valley: its Board of Directors. Literacy Volunteers of America, Inc., is a national literacy organization.

Coordination of our program occurs through the
Family Literacy Advisory Committee.

Advisory Committee members represent the partners who cooperate to provide needed services. The day-to-day operational decisions are made by the agencies responsible for a particular aspect, while overlapping services are determined through group decision. For example, the school district schedules the bus routes. But the coordination with adult and child class schedules is done through consensus of the **Advisory Committee**.

Our Executive Director and Lead Instructors meet regularly with the representatives from social services, the public schools, the YMCA, the technical college, and the adult students to oversee the program. This joint decision-making balances out the distribution of funds. It also brings a wealth of insights and varying perspectives into the program, factors which are crucial to its long term success.

**Consequently,
a well-balanced advisory committee
ensures a more balanced
family literacy program.**

The advisory committee is responsible for keeping all participants focused on the goal of the program: improving the lives of families through education.

Cooperative ventures succeed when partners have had time to work together, develop a shared vision, and feel a sense of ownership. This must happen at all levels.

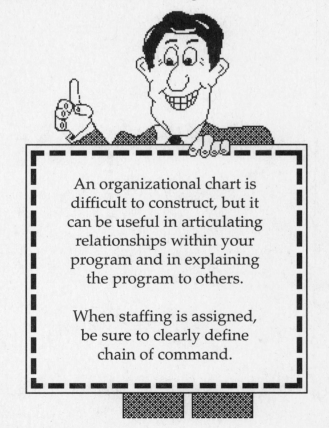

An organizational chart is difficult to construct, but it can be useful in articulating relationships within your program and in explaining the program to others.

When staffing is assigned, be sure to clearly define chain of command.

Organizational Chart
for LVA-CV Family Literacy Program
(See job descriptions, p. 73, for specific roles)

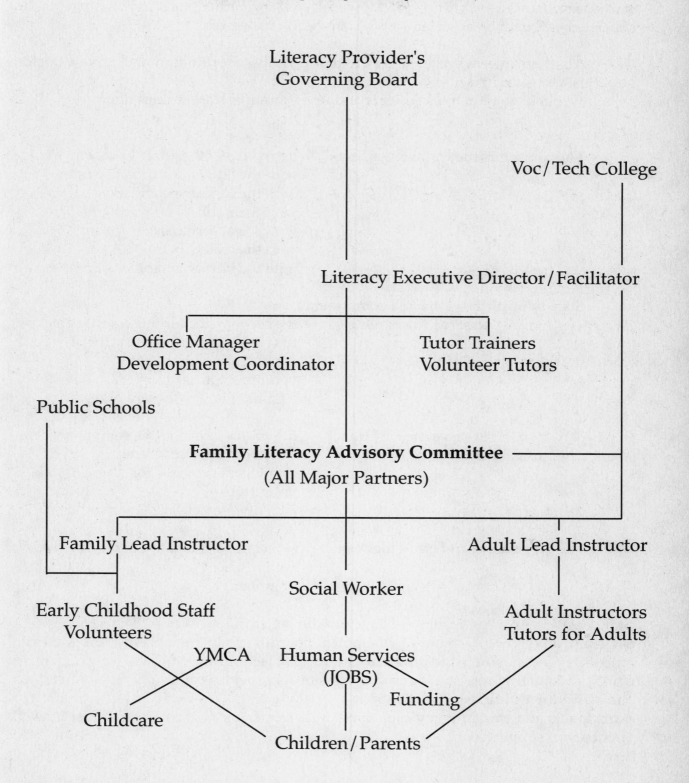

Literacy Provider's
Governing Board

Voc/Tech College

Literacy Executive Director/Facilitator

Office Manager
Development Coordinator

Tutor Trainers
Volunteer Tutors

Public Schools

Family Literacy Advisory Committee
(All Major Partners)

Family Lead Instructor

Adult Lead Instructor

Social Worker

Early Childhood Staff
Volunteers

Adult Instructors
Tutors for Adults

YMCA   Human Services
(JOBS)

Childcare

Funding

Children/Parents

Who coordinates the components?

A **designated coordinator** is essential to efficiency and effective communication within a multifaceted, complex program. However well the caring, conscientious people "in the trenches" function as a team, a program needs leadership.

The job is the same, whether you title this position coordinator, executive director, supervisor, or simply facilitator:
   to oversee all components and keep communication lines open.

This person is the connecting link: between all other staff members
   with the adult education provider
   with the literacy provider
   with the public school systems
   with social services
   with the childcare coordinator
   with the library and other partners

Staff to implement the key components
   to serve the parents: the coordinator for this component
   the basic education instructor
   the parenting instructor
   volunteer tutors
   a family literacy social worker

   to serve the children: the coordinator for this component
   early education teachers
   a childcare provider for siblings
   volunteers
   a family literacy social worker

   for parent and child together: someone to facilitate interaction times
   the preschool teacher
   volunteers

Staff positions can be combined in a number of different ways. The services of a secretary, a bookkeeper, and a development coordinator will also help a program run smoothly. The **size of your program** and **available funding** will help you determine staff. Although a core staff of paid professionals provides continuity, do not overlook the value of **volunteers** to a family literacy team. They can offer support for participants and staff in many capacities. Volunteers, just like paid staff, must be **well trained and supported**.

Day-to-day planning and implementing takes place at all levels. Communication within and among these many levels is essential to teamwork. Schedule time to plan and communicate!

In our program the **Literacy Executive Director** is the overall administrator. Like a team manager, this person keeps an eye on the whole game, from the stands, while recruiting community support. The Executive Director is a connecting link to all partners. (See Appendix 1, p. 80, for a more detailed job description.)

The **Family Literacy Lead Instructor** is the daily coordinator. In our program this person is responsible for:
1. recruiting parents
2. determining families' needs
3. conducting parent orientation
4. teaching group parenting classes
5. supervising preschool and childcare programs (See Appendix 1, p. 77.)
6. arranging home visits

The **Adult Education Lead Instructor** is the adult education coordinator. In our program this person is responsible for:
1. providing adult education instruction
2. facilitating the achievement of parents' academic goals
3. coordinating volunteer hours
4. facilitating career planning (See Appendix 1, p. 75.)

Who will be the key people on your support team?

Study the job descriptions in the Appendix.

Develop job descriptions for both paid and volunteer staff.

Who pays for all this?

A comprehensive family literacy program is an expensive proposition. While federally sponsored grants may be the primary source of funding, the unique cooperation of many different agencies makes operation possible. The program may begin with a little money from many sources. If federal grant money is secured, expansion will be easier. Growth will also come as partners see that integrating their services can be advantageous to all. Everyone benefits, in the long run, when you raise the socio-economic level of the undereducated.

When people ask us where we got the funds in the very beginning, we tell them that we begged or borrowed from every partner we had. It required a lot of creativity and persuasive talking to pull all the pieces together. Having an advisory committee was an advantage, for the members were able to pool the resources of their various agencies. Facilitators working with an existing program may find expanding to a comprehensive model will happen slowly over several years.

Paying for a program without a large grant

From a six-session story hour, we first moved to a small comprehensive program without any large grants. We had a starting budget of less than **$50,000**.

The essential needs were met in this way:

1. Adult education teachers: 20 hours per week provided by vocational/technical college

2. Coordinator/parenting teacher: 20 hours per week provided by public schools: half-time position covered through Chapter 1 funds

3. Preschool teachers: provided by Head Start

4. Childcare on site and books: provided by Junior League volunteers

5. Literacy tutors: provided by volunteers from Literacy Volunteers of America

6. Funding for sibling childcare: through Department of Social Services

7. Supplies and tutor preparation: $3000 Venture grant from United Way

8. Swimming lessons for preschoolers: provided by YMCA

9. Story hours: provided by the public library

What about grants?

It takes a lot of time and expertise to be a successful grant writer. Having an experienced grant writer involved in an advisory capacity can be a valuable asset to your program.

If that isn't possible, start by writing for small local grants to gain some experience.

If you aren't successful, find out what the reviewers had to say. Ask questions of everyone.

If you do obtain a large grant and are concerned about all the paperwork, consider asking one of your partners to act as the fiscal agent. For example, if you apply for an Even Start grant, the public school system or the technical/vocational college might serve as the fiscal agent.

How will you handle your program budget?

You will find guidelines for grant writing on p. 94 and a list of addresses for possible funding on p. 175.

Where to apply for grants:

1. **Local level**
   Call on organizations, such as the United Way, reading councils, publishers, newspapers, and libraries.
   Call on people you know, individuals with similar goals, and retired teachers.
   Seek out potential partners in business and industry.
2. **State level**
   Contact your state department of public instruction.
   Get information from social services, public schools, adult education programs in technical colleges and public schools.
3. **Federal level**
   Go directly to the organizations that distribute federal funds: Chapter 1, Even Start, the Barbara Bush Foundation, etc. See the list and addresses on p. 175.

What if we apply for grants and are turned down?

- Don't give up. Experience is often the best teacher.
- Ask reviewers what elements were missing.
- Go back to where you experienced success and start over.
- Gather statistics to support program growth.
- Seek the advice of your governing board.
- Increase your contacts with businesses, social services, the media, etc.
- Set smaller goals for next year. Take one step at a time.

Example: If you have had a one-to-one adult tutoring program and successful story hour with parents and children six times a year, try adding a six-session parenting and employability class for these families. If childcare for siblings is possible, add that as well, or else work toward that goal in the following year.

From our experience:

From a practical standpoint, we cut down on paperwork by combining forms from the different funders. There are other forms such as information release forms which, if shared between agencies, lead to smoother collaboration and less duplication of services. Appendix 3 (beginning on p. 123) contains samples of the types of forms required to justify financial requests. Adapt them to your own program.

If you aren't proficient on the computer, find a volunteer to help you begin to put this information on a disk. We were able to get a work-study student from the university to process our data. You might also try contacting a professional organization of secretaries in your area for help.

Helpful hints for getting and maintaining consistent funding:

To obtain grants and sustain your funding sources, you must keep accurate statistics. Keeping accurate records from the very beginning will make it easier. This can be a tedious and time-consuming process, but it is necessary. Positive results will enhance funding opportunities. (See Appendix 2, p. 95.) These statistics will also be helpful when it comes time to evaluate your own program.

Important information to document

Adult education number of participants served genders served ages served nationalities prior education occupations hours program was offered hours participants attended assessments and evaluations goals attained	Preschool classes number of participants served genders served ages served ethnic groups hours program was offered hours participants attended assessments and evaluations goals attained
Family unit sibling childcare hours number of siblings	transportation costs percentage of participants using transportation
Parent education hours of participation number served goals met	Parent-child interaction hours of participation number served goals met
Volunteers training hours hours of service retention rate gender, age and occupation	Contributing partners type of agency services provided

To satisfy all partners, you need to document all aspects of the program.

Paying for the more complex program

On the following two pages, you will find examples of some potential ways to cover operating costs in a comprehensive family literacy program. These charts are based on the budgets of our program for 1993-94. Both charts reflect a program operating primarily from acquired federal grant money.

Here are possible funding sources for total operation:

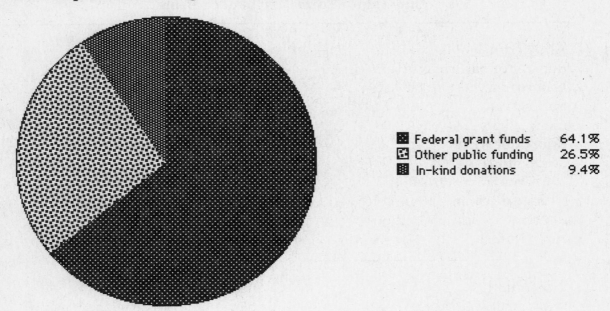

	Federal grant funds	64.1%
	Other public funding	26.5%
	In-kind donations	9.4%

Explanation of categories:

<u>Federal grant funds:</u>   Primarily educational grants, such as Even Start, Head Start, Chapter 1, and Library Services and Construction Act (LSCA)

<u>Other public funding:</u>   Adult education pays the salary of adult instructor and purchases supplies
Public school pays the salary of preschool teacher and purchases supplies
United Way pays the salary of tutor trainer

<u>In-kind donations:</u>   Library space and utilities
Busing through public schools
Classroom assistance of college interns
Time and efforts of literacy tutors
Time and efforts of Junior League volunteers
Time and efforts of hard-working parents

Obtaining an Even Start grant or other large grant could be the first giant step in building a comprehensive program. These federal funds will enable you to expand your existing staff and program. Careful management of grant money can meet many and varied needs.

Here is an example of ways to use Even Start funds in an academic year:

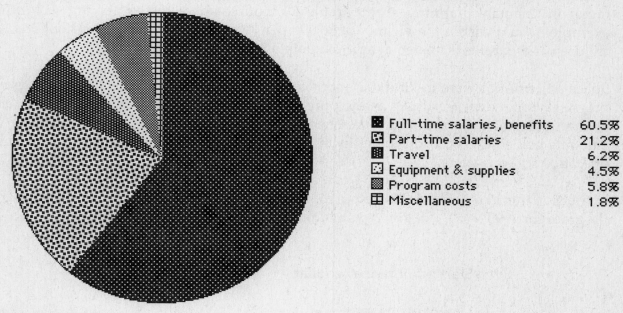

■	Full-time salaries, benefits	60.5%
⊞	Part-time salaries	21.2%
▦	Travel	6.2%
⊠	Equipment & supplies	4.5%
▨	Program costs	5.8%
⊞	Miscellaneous	1.8%

Explanation of categories:

Full-time salaries are for:

Family literacy lead instructor   100 percent
Adult education instructors (grant pays part)
Executive director   (grant pays part)

Part-time salaries are for:

Preschool and childcare teachers
Social worker
Secretary/computer assistant

Travel expenses cover:

Required Even Start training (out of state)
Even Start evaluation (out of state)
State meetings

Equipment and supplies include:

Computer/software
Books
Consumable products

Program costs include other needs:

Telephone service and other utilities
Childcare not covered by JOBS
Some transportation

What does a program like this cost?

The overall price tag of a comprehensive family literacy program such as the one in Eau Claire, Wisconsin, comes to roughly $176,000 to serve fifty families. This figure has been computed by assigning a monetary value to <u>in-kind donations</u> and adding that to the federal grant funds and other sources of public funding. Donations are a significant factor in financial planning. Comparable LVA office space in the private sector, for example, would cost in the vicinity of $6,000 per year. Transportation by school bus for children and parents is valued at approximately $5,400 per year.

Space and utilities were in-kind donations for us, but they could be included in a grant proposal. Some expenses, such as the purchase of equipment and supplies, are greatest at the outset of the program. Other needs fluctuate, depending on the number of students being served. The budget in this manual reflects a program that has been in operation for four years.

The following is a nonspecific itemization of costs in the Eau Claire Family Literacy Program for 1993-94. It will give you an idea of fund distribution.

Even Start grant money available		$ 112,642
Spent on salaries	$ 91,800	
Program maintenance costs	$ 18,500	
Non-federal funds allocated		$ 46,500
In-kind donations (assigned value)		$ 17,500
Total operating expenses (approximate)		**$176,000**

Our annual cost per family in 1993-1994
  based on 50 families
  9 months of service
  for an average of 15 hours per week

$ 3,520

(Includes contributions and in-kind donations)

This figure is consistent with the average program cost per family, serving 30-99 families, given in the 1993 Even Start Report (St. Pierre, 1993). Your budget will reflect the needs and economic conditions of your own area. A flexible budget allows for unforeseen expenditures.

Sample Even Start Budget

Literacy Volunteers of America - Chippewa Valley

Salary and Fringes	Hours	Weeks	
Lead Instructor/Coordinator	100%	36 Weeks	$ 48,692
ABE Instructors*	28%	36 Weeks	$ 7,000
Literacy Executive Director*	25%	40 Weeks	$ 12,130
Total			$ 67, 822

Travel			
Required LVA Training			$ 2,000
Even Start Evaluations and Other Meetings			$ 5,000
Contractual Services			
Preschool Teacher	26 Hours	36 Weeks	$ 7,000
Childcare Teacher	26 Hours	36 Weeks	$ 7,000
Social Worker	15 Hours	34 Weeks	$ 6,120
Workstudy/Computer			$ 1,200
LVA-CV Secretarial			$ 2,500
Computer/Development Coordinator			$ 2,500
YMCA Rent			$ 500
Telephone			$ 500
Sibling Childcare			$ 3,500
Transportation			$ 2,000
Major Equipment (such as furniture -- over $500)			$ 2,000
Supplies Computer ($ 2,000)			
Software, Books, Consumable Products			$ 3,000
Total			$ 44,820
NET TOTAL			$112, 642

Federal Share	$ 112,642
Non-federal Share	$ 46,500
Total	$ 159,142

Detail of Non-federal Share:

*Portion of salaries paid by other sources

ABE Instructors and Literacy Executive Director	$ 37,000
Supplies	$ 2,000
Other: Head Start Teacher from public school	$ 7,500
Total	$ 46,500

Assessment and evaluation:

Why are they important?
How can we assess an existing program?
How do we evaluate a program or key component?

Material in this section contributed by
Dr. John Whooley, University of Wisconsin-Eau Claire

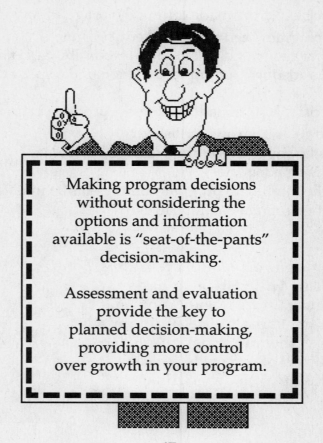

Making program decisions
without considering the
options and information
available is "seat-of-the-pants"
decision-making.

Assessment and evaluation
provide the key to
planned decision-making,
providing more control
over growth in your program.

Why are assessment and evaluation important?

A systematic approach to making decisions in a comprehensive family literacy program is essential. Assessment and evaluation enable the decision-maker to make an informed choice from among options appropriate to the decision.

Assessment involves information-processing. (gathering, organizing, analyzing)	**Evaluation entails determining the merit or worth of all options in a decision.**

Assessment and evaluation are important at all phases of program development.

Examples of decisions to be made in the **planning phase:**
- What should be the program goals?
- What partners should be involved to ensure program success?
- What means should be used to recruit participants?
- What should be included in a volunteer-training program?

Examples of decisions to be made during the **program implementation phase:**
- Has the program been implemented as planned?
- Are the partners carrying out their responsibilities effectively?
- Are funds adequate for implementation of the specific components?

Examples of decisions to be made during the **program certification phase:**
- Have the goals been accomplished?
- Should all components of the program be retained?
- Is the staffing adequate?
- Should the funding of program components be modified?
- Should the program continue to exist?

An evaluation based on your program's predetermined goals will provide a basis for improving the program. An evaluation that incorporates the concerns of the program's partners will assist them in program-related decision-making. It will also provide a means to articulate your success to your financial backers.

How can we assess an existing program?

As you examine your program, you will be asking yourself the following questions:
- Should my program be more comprehensive?
- Is it adequate as it now exists?
- What factors, if any, should be added to my program to enhance its services?

Since needs will change and new resources will become available, it is helpful to periodically reassess all aspects of the program in relationship to your goals.

We have provided a checklist for you to assist in the decision-making regarding the growth and comprehensiveness of your program. It is based on the comprehensive program concept described in this book. (See Appendix 3, Form G.)

Before you use this list, consider your own program goals:
- Are they clearly defined?
- Do they reflect the needs in your community?
- Are they concrete enough to base programs on?
- Are they realistic for your program size and funding?

Then consider the services and components suggested and ask yourself:
- Which exist in your program?
- Which are needed?
- Which would be unrealistic or unnecessary to include at this time?

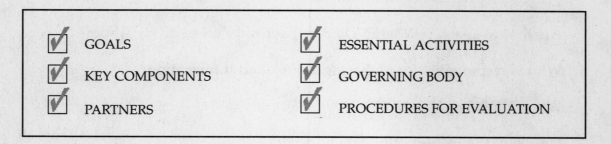

☑ GOALS	☑ ESSENTIAL ACTIVITIES
☑ KEY COMPONENTS	☑ GOVERNING BODY
☑ PARTNERS	☑ PROCEDURES FOR EVALUATION

 After you complete the checklist, go back to it again and make your own list of the items not included in your program. Provide a rationale for the exclusion of each one.

 Make a second list of the items you feel are needed in your program. Assign priority ranking to these items. This will help you establish an implementation time-line.

How do we evaluate a program or key component?

A comprehensive family literacy program that has already been planned and implemented can be evaluated in its entirety by using the following sequential, interrelated steps. These steps may also be applied to the evaluation of a key component.

1. **Who will be making decisions about the program?**

   List the decision-makers: Board of Directors, funding agency, etc.

2. **What decisions regarding the program will they make?**

   These provide direction to the assessment and evaluation procedures.

3. **What options exist with reference to each decision?**

   List the viable options related to each decision. Decision-making is enhanced when **all** options are considered.

4. **What information needs to be collected?**

   The decisions to be made and their options will determine the information needs. For example, if a decision is to be made about program funding, all information relevant to that decision should be obtained.

5. **What information-gathering procedures and/or instruments are needed to provide the necessary information?**

   Are they available? Where? Do they have to be created? By whom?

6. **Who is responsible for gathering the needed information?**

   Where? When? How?

7. **How will the information/data be analyzed?**

   When? By Whom?

8. **How will the results be reported to the decision-makers?**

   When? By whom?

> See Appendix 3, Form H, for a form which may be duplicated.

Some program managers consider assessment and evaluation as unnecessary and time-consuming activities intended to satisfy interested parties. Consequently these tools are sometimes rather thoughtlessly tacked on to the certifying phase of program development.

Our approach stresses the importance of assessment and evaluation to informed, intelligent decision-making. Because that kind of decision-making should take place during the planning and implementing, as well as the certifying phases, of program development, it follows that assessment and evaluation are integral rather than accidental to a well-designed and functioning family literacy program.

We feel that it is difficult to consider assessment and evaluation as unnecessary, time-consuming activities when they are at the heart of the decision-making process.

Where do you stand on this?

Assessment and evaluation resource

For lists, descriptions, and publishers of standardized tests currently available for the components in family literacy, contact:

- Chapter 1 Technical Assistance Center
  Region D/4
  9209 West 110th Street
  Overland Park, KS 66210
  (800)922-9031

- Chapter 1 Technical Assistance Center
  Region C/Test Information Center
  1979 Lakeside Parkway, Suite 400
  Tucker, GA 30084
  (800) 241-3865

Ask for:

- Selected Academic Skills Tests for Adults
- Selected Early Childhood Assessments
- Selected Educational Tests for Speakers of Languages Other than English

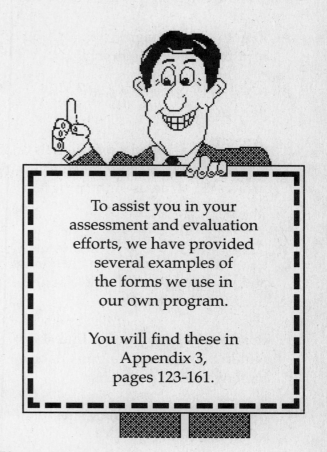

To assist you in your assessment and evaluation efforts, we have provided several examples of the forms we use in our own program.

You will find these in Appendix 3, pages 123-161.

71

By now you should have a clear picture of what a family literacy program is like and what it can do. You also realize that you have not been abandoned to build a family literacy program all alone!

Here are a few final tips for family literacy coordinators to ensure a smoother journey:

A. Plan to spend a significant amount of time in program planning.

B. Build in time to meet with other partners and staff.

C. Seek out the skilled professionals and trained volunteers in your community to assist in all areas of the program.

D. Set realistic goals.

E. Learn from others: attend seminars and conferences with other family literacy professionals.

F. Read everything you can find about family literacy and continue to be a lifelong learner yourself.

G. Visit other family literacy sites.

H. Use the wealth of resources in your community: the media, volunteer groups, university students, and professional organizations.

I. Use the materials and information in the Appendix sections of this manual to make your life easier.

J. Understand that not every family will find success in the program. You can only offer the opportunity; the adults must accept the challenge.

K. Maintain a sense of humor; be flexible and patient.

L. Take a vacation! Get away for a while.

M. **ENJOY THE PROCESS, WITH ALL ITS JOYS AND CHALLENGES!**

Contents of the Appendix Sections

Appendix: Section 1
Sample job descriptions

These generic job descriptions are meant to serve as a guide as you develop job descriptions for each of your family literacy staff members.

Paid, advisory, and volunteer staff are all included.

The job descriptions are based on the format presented in
Maintaining the Balance: A Guide to 50/50 Management (DuPrey, 1992).

It is time-consuming
but important
to lay the groundwork
to establish
everyone's role.

Job descriptions can also help
when it comes time
for evaluations.

ADULT EDUCATION COORDINATOR

Reports to: Vocational/Technical College or Community Education Coordinator
Serves on Family Literacy Advisory Board

Function: Responsible for hiring and supervising adult education instructors and coordinating the adult component of the program

Specific Duties:
1. Serve as link between vocational/technical college or community education source and Family Literacy Advisory Committee
2. Supervise adult education instructors
3. Format adult education curriculum
4. Assist in securing grants and other funding

Qualifications: Determined by hiring agency

ADULT EDUCATION LEAD INSTRUCTOR

Reports to: Adult Education Coordinator

Function: Responsible for assessing students, implementing the adult curriculum, and monitoring student progress

Specific Duties:
1. Assess student abilities
   a. Conduct informal interviews
   b. Administer informal reading inventory or standardized tests
   c. Conduct portfolio assessments
2. Facilitate student progress
   a. Help student define long- and short-term goals
   b. Provide for career planning
   c. Conduct ongoing portfolio assessments
   d. Teach study skills, emphasizing a variety of learning styles
   e. Maintain supportive environment, fostering parent self-esteem
3. Collaborate with other agencies to meet student needs
   a. Coordinate with literacy provider staff to acquire tutors for students needing extra help
   b. Work with tutors to further student goals

       c. Communicate with Family Literacy Social Worker and Family Literacy Coordinator to maintain awareness of student emotional needs
       d. Work with coordinator and preschool teachers to implement parent/child interaction component
       e. Attend staff meetings
4. Complete reports to comply with program requirements
       a. Registration and state reports for Adult Basic Education
       b. Registration and yearly reports for literacy provider
       c. Attendance reports to JOBS
       d. Work with local evaluator to gather statistics
5. Attend staff development opportunities

Qualifications:
1. Master's degree in education
2. Experience with adult education and targeted population
3. Experience with volunteer tutors. (Tutor trainer certification preferred)

CHILDCARE DIRECTOR

Reports to: Hiring agency
               Serves on Family Literacy Advisory Committee

Function: Implement and supervise childcare for siblings of Family Literacy participants

Specific Duties:
1. Implement the childcare for Family Literacy participants
2. Supervise the childcare for Family Literacy participants
3. Complete necessary paperwork to ensure payment for funding for childcare (childcare vouchers, monthly attendance forms, enrollment forms, health forms, etc.)
4. Determine salaries of staff
5. Establish limits on ordering of supplies and consumable materials
6. Provide noon meal and snacks for the Family Literacy children, if part of program

Qualifications: Must meet licensing requirements of state in which program exists

FAMILY LITERACY LEAD INSTRUCTOR/COORDINATOR

Reports to: Adult Education Coordinator
Literacy Provider's Board of Directors (through the Executive
   Director and the Family Literacy Advisory Committee)

Function: Responsible for facilitating daily operational aspects of program

Specific Duties:
   For adults
     1. Recruit students
     2. Coordinate support services
       a. Childcare needs
       b. Transportation needs
       c. Referral of crisis situations to Social Worker
     3. Facilitate and implement parenting curriculum
     4. Coordinate efforts with adult education Instructor

   For children
     1. Preschool
       a. Oversee enrollment of students
       b. Coordinate efforts with early childhood education and English
         as a Second Language teachers
       c. Meet legal licensing requirements
     2. Sibling childcare
       a. Monitor and support childcare teacher
       b. Meet legal requirements
     3. Train, schedule, and oversee classroom volunteers

   For parent/child interaction component
     1. Schedule and supervise parent involvement in classrooms
     2. Plan and implement monthly interaction activities

   For Family Literacy Program in general
     1. Fiscal
       a. Work with Executive Director to provide evaluation and
         accountability, as required by grants and partners
       b. Assist Literacy Provider with grant writing and revision
     2. Liaison and promotional
       a. Serve on Family Literacy Advisory Committee
       b. Attend and present at conferences
       c. Assist others in beginning Family Literacy Programs when time
         permits

Qualifications:
1. B. S. degree in elementary education
2. Master's degree in early childhood special education
3. Early childhood teaching experience
4. Childcare services instructor experience
5. Adult education instructor experience

General Comments:

A full-time overseer is essential to a comprehensive family literacy program. There needs to be someone maintaining ongoing contact with participating agencies and providing on-the-scene direction.

FAMILY LITERACY SOCIAL WORKER

Reports to: Family Literacy Program Lead Instructor

Function: To meet immediate social services needs within the program

Specific duties:
1. Work with teacher and staff to develop most beneficial literacy experience for student
2. Meet with each student personally to do family mapping: determining the student's support system, needs, goals, and barriers to those goals
3. Take personal problems out of the classroom, enabling teachers to teach (crisis intervention)
4. Maintain contact with social services and JOBS case workers

Qualifications:
1. Degree in social work
2. Experience with at-risk families
3. Flexibility

General Comments:

The Social Worker does not participate in recruitment, only retention of people accepted to program. A good working relationship with JOBS and social services is essential; special needs are referred to the proper agencies. The Social Worker deals with ordinary day-to-day problems, communicating with authorities and providing a support system with follow-through. Because this is an at-risk group, needing constant monitoring and reinforcement, this position eases the burden on the coordinator by assuming the role of personal counselor.

JOBS CASE MANAGER — SOCIAL SERVICES

Reports to: Hiring agency for social services

Function: Provide vocational testing to determine client options
Provide employment and training services that allow the client to become economically independent

Specific Duties:

1. Refer qualified clients to the Family Literacy Program
2. Provide supportive services
   a. Transportation funding
   b. Childcare funding
   c. Counseling
3. Maintain communication with Family Literacy Social Worker and Family Literacy Lead Instructors
4. Act as resource person for other community services

JOBS REPRESENTATIVE — SOCIAL SERVICES

Reports to: Hiring agency

Function: Supervise implementation of JOBS Program in the area
Act as a link between JOBS case managers and Family Literacy administration

Specific Duties:

1. Link social services agency with other partners
2. Supervise support services:
   a. Oversee daycare and transportation arrangements
   b. Assist case managers in placement of clients
   c. Make sure program goals mesh with goals of literacy provider and client
   d. Evaluate appropriateness of new policies to program
3. Serve on Family Literacy Advisory Committee
4. Link clients to services available in the community and through social services (outside of JOBS)
5. Promote program through presentations to interested parties

LITERACY DEVELOPMENT COORDINATOR

Reports to: Literacy Provider Executive Director
               Adult Education Coordinator

Function: Generate publicity for family literacy and provide computer training and assistance for staff, tutors and students

Specific Duties:
1. Generate publicity for the Family Literacy program
2. Assist adult education instructors, tutors, and students with computer literacy and programming
3. Coordinate development of the literacy movement in area served
4. Act as a spokesperson for the organization
5. Design and facilitate literacy promotions and special events

Qualifications:
1. Extensive knowledge of the community
2. Experience as a literacy volunteer
3. High school diploma — college background preferred
4. Specific technical and interpersonal skills
   a. Excellent organizational ability
   b. Excellent communication skills
   c. Computer knowledge and ability to teach computer literacy
   d. Understanding of needs and problems of adult learners

LITERACY EXECUTIVE DIRECTOR/ADMINISTRATOR

Reports to: Literacy Provider's Board of Directors
               Adult Education Coordinator

Function: Coordinate the family literacy effort within the area served

Specific Duties:
1. Act as a coordinating link to bring interested parties together to promote family literacy
2. Act as administrator of federal grant funding for Board of Directors

3. Appoint a representative from the Board of Directors to serve on the Family Literacy Advisory Committee
4. Maintain educational integrity of the program
5. Help seek additional funding (grant writing)
6. Promote the program at the local, state and national levels
7. Assist Tutor Coordinator (of literacy office) in training and supporting volunteers who tutor adult students in the program
8. Work with other volunteer groups to assist the program
9. Guide future direction of Family Literacy Program

Qualifications:
1. Bachelor's degree in education
2. Master's degree in reading
3. Meet licensing and certification requirements
4. Experience in teaching adults and children
5. Extensive knowledge of community through community service and job experience
6. Supervisory experience
7. Experience in training and supporting volunteers in literacy programs
8. Extensive grant writing experience
9. Consulting experience in Family Literacy at the state level

General Comments:
This position demands:
1. knowledge of educational programming for adults and children to maintain the educational integrity of the program
2. knowledge of educational programming for training and support of volunteers working with adult students
3. flexibility
4. the desire to exert much time and energy into building a program
5. willingness to be the responsible party — the one following through on all decisions, completing grant applications, calling meetings and monitoring progress of the program
6. knowledge of community resources and existing services to prevent duplication of services
7. the ability to communicate in writing and orally at the local, state, and national level regarding Family Literacy

LITERACY OFFICE MANAGER

Reports to: Executive Director of literacy provider

Function: Secretarial and organizational assistance to program
(This could be part-time if just for family literacy, or possibly filled by a work study student from a nearby college.)

Specific Duties:
1. Be responsible for compilation and submission of reports for partners and grant procurement
2. Provide clerical assistance using "state of the art" computer techniques
3. Do office bookkeeping, including writing checks, deposits, payroll
4. Schedule appointments for personnel
5. Answer telephone and communicate messages
6. Meet, introduce, arrange rooms for tutors and students

Qualifications:
1. Experience with computerized office
2. Experience with volunteer groups
3. High school/college preparation in area of information processing with computer emphasis
4. Specific technical and interpersonal skills
   a. Excellent ability to communicate orally and in writing
   b. Ability to meet and greet the public in warm, professional manner
   c. Ability to perform in busy, sometimes hectic, environment
   d. Excellent word processing skills
   e. Willingness to learn about the adult learner and volunteer tutor

PRESCHOOL TEACHER

Reports to: Hiring agency (such as public schools or other Head Start
                   administrator)
              Family Literacy Program Lead Instructor
              Family Literacy Adult Education Lead Instructor

Function: To provide education for preschoolers and facilitate parent/child
              interaction component

Specific Duties:

1. Provide positive experience in all areas of development for preschool
   child
   a. Language-based learning environment for age-appropriate skills
   b. Cooperative emphasis for developing social skills and
      communication
   c. PLAN-DO-REVIEW* approach for cognitive skills and continuity
   d. Art activities for creative expression
   e. Physical activities for gross-motor skills
   f. Hands-on activities for fine-motor skills
2. Plan and assist with parent/child interaction time in the classroom
   setting and in monthly interaction activities
3. Share information with Adult Education Instructor and Family
   Literacy Social Worker to assist student's family
4. Assist Adult Education Instructor with adult education
5. Supervise transportation of children between programs and sites
6. Facilitate integration with Chapter 1 programs when needed

Qualifications:

1. Meets all state certification requirements for childcare/preschool
2. Has bachelor's degree in education
3. Has experience in early childhood/adult education

General Comments:

This is a multifaceted position that has evolved according to program
needs. It is necessary for this individual to have sufficient training and
background to fill a variety of roles. Specific duties are determined by
program enrollment and space capabilities. The preschool agenda
follows the designated curriculum.

* High/ Scope Curriculum, Ypsilanti, MI, 1979

SPECIAL SERVICES DIRECTOR -- PUBLIC SCHOOLS

Reports to: Hiring agency

Function: To act as the Family Literacy link with the school district
               To serve on the Family Literacy Advisory Committee

Specific Duties:
1. Resource person — using existing programs (such as Head Start) when they can be used to meet needs of both groups
2. Grant writing — assisting Family Literacy Advisory Committee in securing funding
3. Physical needs — providing classroom space in school buildings
4. Transportation — providing busing for eligible participants and their children
5. Positive support — fostering within the school district an attitude supportive of family literacy endeavor
6. Communication — forwarding information relative to the Family Literacy initiative to appropriate school employees, including school board members

TUTOR TRAINER/READING CONSULTANT

Reports to: Literacy Provider Executive Director

Function: To provide tutor training and support

Specific Duties:
1. Assist with tutor training
2. Support tutors and students during tutoring period
3. Maintain contact with ABE teachers in Family Literacy program
4. Provide in-service for tutors at the Family Literacy sites
5. Assist Executive Director as projects develop

Qualifications:
1. College degree with strong emphasis in field of reading
2. Experience in teaching adults: special education, learning disabilities, English as a Second Language
3. Experience as a literacy volunteer and working with community groups

4. Ability to communicate well orally and in writing with diverse activities and individuals
5. Concern for helping functional illiterates and an understanding of the needs and problems of the adult learner
6. Computer literacy

VOLUNTEER — JUNIOR LEAGUE

Reports to: Literacy Provider staff and Adult Education Instructors for tutoring
Family Literacy Lead Instructor for childcare
Literacy Provider Development Coordinator for library
In-service conducted by Family Literacy Lead Instructor

Specific Duties:
1. Assist staff in children's room
2. Tutor adult students
3. Act as librarian for literacy library
4. Provide progress reports to Literacy Provider staff

VOLUNTEER TUTOR

Reports to: Literacy Provider
                Adult Education Instructors

Function: To tutor adult learners in basic skills

Specific Duties:
1. Maintain confidentiality regarding assigned student
2. Actively prepare for each session
3. Maintain records of tutoring sessions
4. Maintain contact with the literacy provider staff concerning the student's progress
5. Arrange meetings with the student in a public building or work with the Adult Education Instructor in charge of the adult classroom
6. Follow the guidance of the Adult Education Instructor in charge of the adult classroom
7. Adhere to the goals and procedures of literacy provider

Qualifications:
1. Must have a sincere desire to help other adults develop their reading and writing skills
2. Must have completed required tutor training
3. Must make a commitment to attend inservices and training sessions
4. Must be willing to tutor a student for a minimum of six to nine months

Rights of a Tutor:
1. To be viewed as a valuable resource to this agency, its staff, and its clients
2. To be given meaningful assignments, with full involvement and participation
3. To be treated as an equal with coworkers
4. To have effective supervision
5. To receive recognition for work done

Appendix: Section 2
Tools you can't do without

The challenges of any new endeavor are always simplified somewhat if you can take advantage of the trial-and-error knowledge of those who have gone before you.

In this section we have included information useful when assessing the need for family literacy within a community. The facts and statistics you collect will be important to potential funders. We have also included samples of the materials we have used for publicity and distribution of information. As stated earlier, the more professional your press releases and brochures, the better your first impression will be among those whom you are trying to reach.

You will find the following **information** and **samples** on the pages given:

Puzzle Tool
A conceptual tool created as an aid to program development

Family Literacy, Piece by Piece
Created by the Family Literacy team, LVA-CV
Eau Claire, Wisconsin
Used in LVA National Family Literacy Institute
October 1993

A family literacy program begins with parents and children

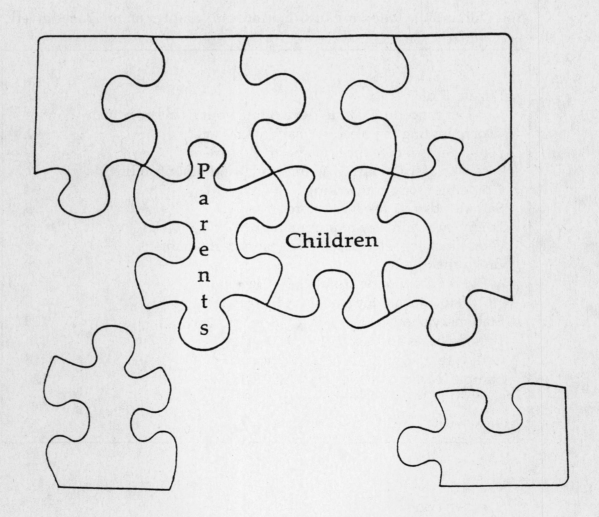

**The next step is to fill in the pieces you need.
Consider the basic components:**

**Education for the adult
Education for the preschoolers
Parent education
Parent/child interaction**

What pieces do you already have? What pieces are you missing?

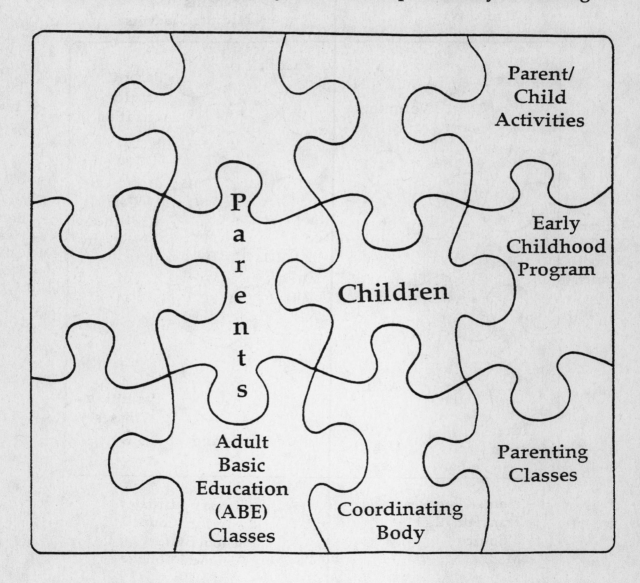

What about a site?   **Child care?**   **Funding sources?**
Other partners?   **Volunteers?**   **Volunteers?**

There are many variations
of a comprehensive literacy program.
This is one example:

- Grants
  (Ex. Even Start)
- Donations
- United Way

- Literacy Tutors
- Junior League
- College Education
  Students
- Childcare Students

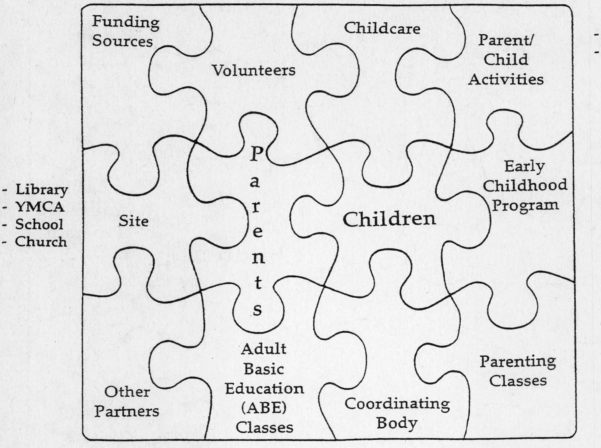

- Library
- YMCA
- School
- Church

- Home-Based
- Classroom
  Interaction

- Preschool
- Head Start
- Chapter 1
- Story Hour

- Human Services
- Transportation
  Source
- Media

- Literacy Affiliate
- Advisory Council
- School System
- Technical College

**Here is a blank puzzle
to help you visualize and assess
your own family literacy program.**

Documenting the Need for Family Literacy

A report compiled by: Wayne Atkins, 1994 President of the LVA-CV Board of Directors and Kathy Brunstad, Lead Instructor for Family Literacy Adult Education

In planning for a family literacy program, as is the case for any organization delivering a service to a segment of a community, the gathering and analysis of demographic data are imperative.

While the Federal Bureau of the Census represents the base source of demographic data, within a year or two of each decennial census, many compilations and analyses of such data will already have been done. In many cases, other organizations with missions that parallel those of literacy providers will have gathered and tabulated demographic data in a form useable with virtually no changes required.

In Wisconsin the Board of the State Technical College System, in cooperation with the Statewide Basic Skills Task Force, has published *Selected Student, Staff, and Performance Data*, a statistical report filled with the type of demographic data useful to any literacy provider. In addition, many of the state's technical colleges have refined these data to make them applicable to their respective communities. Absent these sources, the Wisconsin Department of Administration publishes the *Wisconsin Bluebook*, an annual update of statistical information relating to the demographics, economy, and other aspects of trends within the state. Other states have similar publications that can be obtained by contacting state officials.

Once the sources of data for a service area have been located, they should be tabulated over time; e.g., two or three 10-year intervals. This should establish trends such as the percent of increases/decreases. In addition, subdivisions of the area served (e.g., counties, cities and other areas) should be shown with their respective trends. This will enable the literacy provider to more easily ensure geographic equality in the provision of its services.

Specific trends the Literacy Volunteers of America-Chippewa Valley found useful in developing the demographic report that served as the basis for its Strategic Plan are:
1. Population trends, by county and state
2. Minority population trends, by county and state
3. Current population by gender, by county and state
4. Educational level of adults 25 years or older, by county
5. Other than English spoken at home, by county and state
6. Population 25 years or older, by age categories, by county

Note that most of these demographics include the state as a basis for comparison. This should enable the literacy provider to ascertain which characteristics of its service area are atypical with respect to the state in which it is located.

Shown below are two of the specific tables, together with their analyses, that were developed for the Chippewa Valley affiliate of LVA and that served as the basis for many of the assumptions included in its 1994 strategic plan.

TABLE 2: MINORITY POPULATION TRENDS BY COUNTY AND STATE

COUNTY	YEAR 1970	1980	1990	PERCENT OF CHANGE 1970-80	1970-90
Chippewa	111	284	620	155.9	458.6
Dunn	178	493	1,090	177.0	512.4
Eau Claire	354	914	3,244	158.2	816.4
TOTAL	643	1,691	4,954	163.0	670.5
Wisconsin	158,974	262,732	472,440	65.3	197.2

This table shows the rather dramatic increase in the minority make-up of LVA-CV's service area. The total of 643 in 1970 represented only 0.4 percent of the total population whereas the 4,954 minority residents in 1990 raised this proportion to nearly 3 percent. The minority make-up of LVA-CV's service area has increased at nearly 3 1/2 times the corresponding increase for the state of Wisconsin.

TABLE 4: EDUCATIONAL LEVEL OF ADULTS BY COUNTY

COUNTY	0-8 NUMBER	%	9-12 NUMBER	%	0-12 NUMBER	%	TOTAL
Chippewa	4,423	13.3	3,900	11.8	8,323	25.1	33,189
Dunn	2,472	12.6	1,941	9.7	4,413	22.4	19,672
Eau Claire	4,271	8.7	4,220	8.6	8,491	17.2	49,259
TOTAL	11,166	10.9	10,061	9.9	21,277	20.8	102,120

Table 4 indicates that more than one in ten adults in the LVA-CV service area have eight years or less of formal education and more than one in five did not complete a high school education. While the more rural counties reflect a somewhat higher rate of non-completion, Eau Claire County still manifests a non high-school graduation rate of more than 17 percent.

These tables represent a sample of the demographic statistics you may need to compile.

Guidelines for grant writing

The following tips are taken from *Grant Writing from A to Z*, by Teresa Sweeney.

Basics

1. Write simply and clearly. (This can't be said enough.)
2. Use positive, expressive, action-oriented statements instead of passive, vague language.
3. Do not use jargon. Do not use acronyms unless you have spelled out the words they stand for. (In other words, do not assume the reader knows the lingo or the field.)
4. Use quantitative information whenever possible.
5. Verify all monetary quotes. Check your budget figures with a calculator!
6. Perform a "checks and balances" on the content. Do all parts of the proposal relate to each other? Is the information in each part in logical order? Is it coherent?
7. The idea for a proposal may be developed by a group, but the proposal should be written by one or two people.
8. Keep draft versions of the" boilerplate" [sample for reference] and new projects handy so you can quickly produce a proposal when funding opportunities arise. Then, tailor your request to the specific guidelines of each funder.
9. Do not exceed the number of pages requested (and don't try to stretch it by attaching 30 pages of appendices!).
10. Format should be double-spaced, consistent (headings, indents, etc.), and easy on the eye.

Golden Rules

1. Make sure your proposal fits the mission and desires of the funder.
2. Follow the guidelines, instructions and format to the letter.
3. Write simply and clearly. PROOFREAD the final version, please!
4. Submit before the deadline, if possible. If you are within a day or two of the deadline, deliver it by hand or by overnight mail.
5. When creating a proposal from scratch, double the amount of time you think it will take. When tailoring a boilerplate proposal, add a few days.

Distributed through the United Way of America
Education and Literacy Initiative
Washington, DC — November 1993

Sample abstract for a grant proposal:
Literacy Volunteers of America-Chippewa Valley

The purpose of this application is to secure funds with which to remodel and expand the current Family Literacy Program into the <u>Equal Opportunities in Literacy Through Even Start</u> project as proposed herein. It is anticipated that this project, which will serve as a national Even Start model (as was the case with its parent Family Literacy Program), will serve seventy-five (75) families, including seventy-five (75) adults and one hundred twenty (120) children. These families will include those in which the parents are eighteen (18) years or older, one or both do/does not have a high school diploma or demonstrate(s) a basic literacy need, and with one or more children between the ages of three (3) to seven (7) years, residing in a Chapter One school attendance area to enroll in an early education program.

The outcomes expected to emanate from this project are:

1.   Children's school readiness and literacy-related skills will be increased as they reach their full potential as learners.

2.   Parents' functional literacy skills, general education, career awareness, and computer literacy skills will be raised through ABE instruction and career planning workshops.

3.   Parents will acquire a greater understanding of child growth and development, skill in applying positive child guidance techniques, and greater awareness of their role as the primary teacher of their children in providing a home environment that supports children's learning and strengthened family relationships in the areas of wellness and fitness.

4.   Collaboration between local organizations, the Department of Human Services, and educational agencies providing services to young children will be increased.

5.   A model Even Start program which will be in demand for replication on a statewide and national level will be developed.

In summary, although the Eau Claire community through Literacy Volunteers of America-Chippewa Valley has become known nationally for its Family Literacy Program, its current activity level equals or exceeds its available resources, and before it can implement this desperately needed Even Start project which is proposed herein, LVA-CV must obtain funding.

Even Start eligibility requirements

The following information is specific to Even Start funding but may also prove helpful when establishing your own guidelines or pursuing other grants.

Eligible Even Start participants are:
1. parents who are eligible for adult education under the Adult Education Act and who have an eligible child
2. parents whose eligible children, ages birth through 7, reside in an elementary school attendance area participating in the basic Chapter 1 program

At least one parent and child from each family must participate together in the Even Start program.

To be an eligible Even Start participant, an adult must be:
1. the "parent" of an eligible child (as defined above)

   "Parent" includes, in addition to a biological or adoptive parent, a legal guardian or other person standing "in loco parentis." Generally, "in loco parentis" means a person acting in place of a parent or legal guardian, and may include a person such as a grandparent, stepparent, aunt, uncle, older sibling, or other person either (1) with whom the child lives or (2) who has been designated by a parent, legal guardian, or court to act in place of the parent, legal guardian, or court regarding all aspects of the child's education.

2. eligible for participation in an adult education program under the Adult Education Act, 20 U.S.C. 1201 (a) (1) and (2).

Eligible adults under the Adult Education Act are:
1. at least 16 years old or beyond the age of compulsory school attendance of the particular state
2. not enrolled in a secondary school
3. lacking sufficient basic educational skills to function effectively in society or do not have a certificate of graduation from a school providing secondary education and have not achieved an equivalent level of education
4. not currently required to be enrolled in schools
5. impaired in their ability to get or retain employment by their inability to speak, read, or write the English language

Guidelines for selection of Even Start participants:

The challenge in any community is to identify and serve those eligible participants most in need of the activities and services. Section 1056 (c) (5) (a) of the act (Even Start Family Literacy Program Statute) requires that projects receiving Even Start Family Literacy funds make every effort to serve the most needy in their community. Whether or not a project will be able to select all eligible children and their parents, participants should be selected through a fair and objective process. The following process (suggested in nonregulatory guidance by the U. S. Department of Education in 1992) may be used as a general guideline:

1. Prepare a clear explanation of the statutory and regulatory eligibility criteria, including an explanation of the criteria that will be used by the project to identify those participants most in need of Even Start activities and services.

2. Disseminate information about the program and eligibility criteria to the public and appropriate cooperating agencies.

3. Actively identify and recruit eligible participants.

4. Select families most in need from the eligible pool using a defined process (e.g., rank-ordering, weighting, or additional criteria).

5. Screen and prepare parents and children selected for participation, by arranging, as necessary, for assessment, counseling, or other developmental and support services such as special education or nutritional or medical services.

This information and the Even Start eligibility criteria listed on page 90 were provided by Monica Notaro, Chapter 1 coordinator of the Wisconsin Department of Public Instruction.

Brochures

The following pages contain a sampling of brochures used to inform parents, partners, and the public about our family literacy program.

Some are from early stages and some depict the current comprehensive offerings.

The next page is a basic description of a comprehensive program, intended for parents who might be considering the program. This page could be copied, with your own information added to the bottom of the sheet, and then given to parents.

FAMILY LITERACY

What is it?

Family Literacy is a comprehensive program that allows parents to return to school to improve their skills and provides an educational experience for their preschool children at the same time.

For the Parent:
Basic education classes
Career planning
Parenting education
Transportation
Childcare for siblings

For the Preschooler:
Reading readiness, learning
how to get along in school

For Parent and Child Together:
An opportunity to enjoy learning, together

Family Literacy is a team effort -- community agencies working together to find ways to solve the problems parents face when they need to further their education or get a better job. With the support of these agencies, trained staff and volunteers, education becomes affordable and productive. Parents are then able to take responsibility for meeting their own goals.

For more information call:

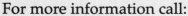

Family
Literacy
Program

Literacy Volunteers of America-Chippewa Valley
Eau Claire, Wisconsin

Parental involvement is a key to childhood development.

Students and tutors work together.

Expanding Literacy Through Learning

The Family Literacy Program has its roots in a literacy effort which began in the Eau Claire area a number of years ago.

In 1986, the Literacy Volunteers of America-Chippewa Valley (LVA-CV) was organized to combat adult illiteracy in Eau Claire, Dunn, and Chippewa counties in west central Wisconsin. LVA-CV operates as an outreach center of Chippewa Valley Technical College (CVTC). LVA-CV cooperates with other organizations and service providers to offer free one-to-one literacy instruction to the adults of this region. The LVA-CV staff trains volunteer tutors, identifies and screens students, recommends suitable tutoring sites, and provides instructional assistance and materials tailored to the student's individual needs. The office is located in the L.E. Phillips Memorial Public Library, 400 Eau Claire Street, Eau Claire, Wisconsin.

In 1988-89, LVA-CV focused its efforts on parents needing literacy services and their preschool children. The needs of this group were addressed through an intergenerational story hour program. LVA-CV's goals for this program were to provide these parents and preschool children with a positive learning experience by sharing books in the public library. Parents enrolled in a literacy program to improve their basic skills.

The Model

Encouraged by the success of the intergenerational story hour program, a comprehensive model developed. The goal of the Family Literacy Program is similar to the story hour: to break the intergenerational cycle of functional illiteracy by uniting parents and their preschool children in a positive educational and recreational experience.

In 1989, the Family Literacy Program was established at the YMCA for Human Services JOBS Program participants. In 1990, a second program was opened in partnership with the Eau Claire public school system. This program is currently located at Lowes Creek Integrated Learning Center in Eau Claire. This is the learning site for Head Start, Chapter One, and Early Childhood Special Needs families. The families spend nine to eighteen hours in class each week. This collaborative effort is funded and administered by LVA-CV, CVTC, Human Services, L.E. Phillips Memorial Public Library, YMCA, United Way, Eau Claire Public Schools, and private donations. Additional funding through the Even Start Grant also enables other families in the community to receive services even though they are not part of the JOBS Program or currently enrolled in a school program.

> **This Family Literacy Program has served over 200 families since 1988 and has been recognized as a state and national model.**

The Younger Generation

The Family Literacy Program provides quality early learning. Professionally trained teachers of early childhood education, using the High Scope curriculum, provide children with an environment which encourages decision making, and fosters creativity and independent thinking. The Family Literacy Program develops prereading and language skills.

The YMCA provides swimming lessons and various creative activities for the children. Childcare services for younger siblings are provided at both sites. Scholarships from the YMCA's Partnership with Youth Program allow parents and children in the Family Literacy Program to use the YMCA facilities during their free time.

Caring teachers encourage children to learn.

Childcare is provided at the YMCA for young siblings.

Children have fun in the YMCA pool.

People of all ages enjoy reading.

Goal Setting for Parents

Individual instruction is provided for parents in the Family Literacy Program by Adult Basic Education instructors from Chippewa Valley Technical College. Instructors evaluate each student by the use of a portfolio assessment and assist in setting educational goals with each individual. These goals are assessed and redefined as each student progresses during the program. LVA tutors are available to assist the adult students.

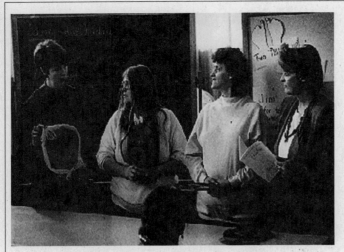

Learning takes place in the classroom.

Parents and Children Working Together

A parental skills component is an important part of the Family Literacy Program curriculum. Each day, special time is provided to enhance the parent/child relationship through planned and structured interaction. Areas covered include child guidance techniques, child development, health and nutrition, and stress management. Each area builds self-esteem and helps empower families.

Parents have an opportunity to help in the early childhood classroom on a monthly basis, and parent/child at home activities are provided. Parents and children can also participate in the local public library story hour. The literacy office is located in the lower level of the public library, where Family Literacy participants feel comfortable and familiar with the environment.

For More Information

Carol Gabler, Executive Director
Literacy Volunteers of America-Chippewa Valley
L.E. Phillips Memorial Public Library
(715)834-0222

Karol Machmeier, Coordinator
Family Literacy Program
(715)836-8460, Ext. 31 (Mon., Wed., and Fri.)
(715)839-2826 (Tues. and Thurs.)

Jack O'Connell, ABE Coordinator
Chippewa Valley Technical College
(715)833-6349

Richard Savolainen, Director of Special Programs
Eau Claire Area Schools System
(715)833-3442

Joanne Tews, JOBS Program Supervisor
Department of Human Services

Volunteers Add a Special Dimension

Volunteers are an important component in the Family Literacy Program. The volunteers include LVA-CV tutors and board members, Junior League members at the preschool sites and the LVA office, university students, Chippewa Valley Technical College childcare students, and other community volunteers.

LVA volunteers participate in a fourteen-hour training program and make a commitment to work with an adult student twice a week, for six to nine months. Tutors can choose to work in the Adult Basic Education classroom or independently with students.

Junior League are trained volunteers who maintain the library collection for LVA, tutor adult students, and work with children in the preschool classes on a weekly basis.

Members from the community, like those involved in the United Way, spend many hours raising funds to support LVA-CV programs.

Volunteers are an important part of Family Literacy.

Program Admission Policy

Family Literacy Program Admission Policy

Applicants for the Family Literacy Program will be accepted based on need. Adults Participating must:
- be at least 18 years of age
- have an interest in improving literacy and educational skills
- have a child age eight or younger residing in a Chapter One school district

Family

Literacy

Program

 Literacy Volunteers of America-Chippewa Valley
Eau Claire, Wisconsin

General Information

The Literacy Volunteers of America-Chippewa Valley Family Literacy Program offers a unique opportunity for parents and children to learn and grow together during the school year. While children attend a quality preschool, Head Start or Early Education program, parents attend Adult Basic Education classes.

Working at an individual pace, parents improve skills in reading, math and writing, and/or prepare for their GED or High School Equivalency tests. Computer training, career planning, and job-seeking skills are also included in this program. Trained tutors are available for the students.

A group "Family Focus" time is provided on a regular basis to help parents understand their children's development and guide their children's behavior to strengthen families.

There are currently two program sites: one at the Lowes Creek Integrated Learning Center and one at the YMCA. Both provide childcare for younger children. The program is free for eligible families.

This program operates under LVA-CV's Board of Directors. This program is funded by LVA, Chippewa Valley Technical College, Eau Claire Department of Human Services, public schools, YMCA, L.E. Phillips Library, United Way, an Even Start Grant, and other donations.

**LOWES
CREEK**

**Tuesday,
Wednesday,
and
Thursday**

**9:00 A.M.
to
3:30 P.M.**

A day of learning is about to begin.

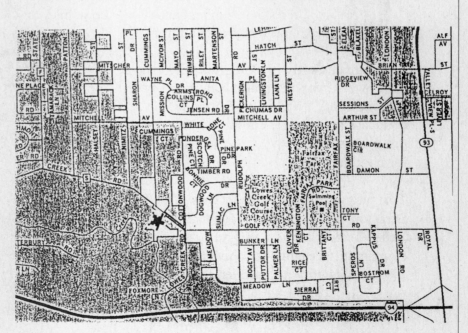

The Lowes Creek Integrated Learning Center is located at 1029 East Lowes Creek Road.

Lowes Creek Family Literacy

Who is Eligible?

Parents who desire to improve basic literacy and educational skills and who have a child in Head Start, Early Childhood Special Education, or kindergarten, in an Eau Claire public school. ESL students with good conversational skills are also eligible.

Note: Parents, with children under age three who are not enrolled in one of the above programs, are eligible provided there is space available.

Classes for parents meet Tuesday, Wednesday, and Thursday during the school year from 9:00 A.M. to 3:30 P.M. in an Adult Basic Education classroom, located on the second floor of Lowes Creek School. Children attend their regular school program.

 Parents who have children attending school at the Lowes Creek Integrated Learning Center may ride the school bus with their child. Other parents may ride the city bus or provide their own transportation.

Childcare is provided for children ages three to five. Other sites offer sibling childcare for children under age three, with some funding available.

All parents may receive additional help from an LVA tutor if they request it. Families enrolled in the Family Literacy Program receive free YMCA family memberships. All parents are encouraged to volunteer in their child's classroom and will have an opportunity to use at-home parent packs with their child.

YMCA

**Monday,
Wednesday,
and
Friday**

**9:00 A.M.
to
2:45 P.M.**

Swimming is provided at the YMCA site.

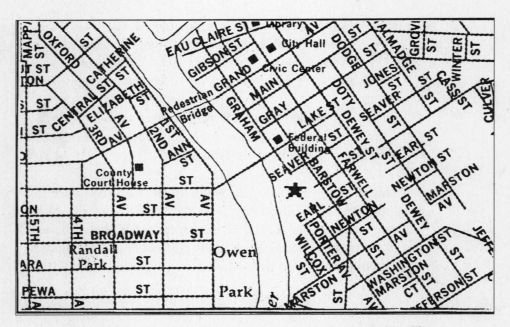

The YMCA is located at 700 Graham Avenue in downtown Eau Claire.

YMCA Family Literacy

Who is Eligible?
Parents who desire to improve basic literacy and educational skills and who have a child between the ages of three and five. Parents who are participating in the JOBS program through the Eau Claire County Department of Human Services and those attending full days will be given priority. ESL students with good conversational skills are also eligible.

Classes for parents and children meet Monday, Wednesday, and Friday from 9:00 A.M. to 2:45 P.M. during the school year. Children attend the Family Literacy Preschool Program during these times in a preschool room in the YMCA. The parents' Adult Basic Education classroom is located next door in the Masonic Temple. Parents in this program must attend all three days!

 Parents may ride the city bus or provide their own transportation, but they will receive some allowance for transportation through the JOBS program.

Childcare for younger siblings is provided at the YMCA for children under age three.

Parents may receive additional help from an LVA tutor if they wish. All families enrolled in the Family Literacy Program receive YMCA Family memberships. Parents are encouraged to volunteer in the preschool room and will receive at-home activity packs to use with their child.

Program Admission Policy

Family Literacy Program Admission Policy
Applicants for the Family Literacy Program will be accepted based on need.
Adults Participating must:
- be at least 18 years of age
- have an interest in improving literacy and educational skills
- have a child age eight or younger residing in a Chapter One school district
- make a commitment to attend classes on a regular basis

For More Information

Karol Machmeier, Lead Instructor
Family Literacy Program
(715)836-8474

Carol Gabler, Executive Director
Literacy Volunteers of America-Chippewa Valley
L.E. Phillips Memorial Public Library
(715)834-0222

Jack O'Connell, ABE Coordinator
Chippewa Valley Technical College
(715)833-6349

Richard Savolainen, Director of Special Programs
Eau Claire Area Schools System
(715)833-3442

Joanne Tews, JOBS Program Supervisor
Department of Human Services
(715)833-1977

Photos by David Joles
Copyright © 1993 Literacy Volunteers of America-Chippewa Valley

112

FAMILY LITERACY
PROGRAM

Cooperating Partners:

Eau Claire County
Department of Human Services

If you are just beginning to organize a comprehensive program, it might be helpful to get a post office box. Correspondence directed to one location avoids a lot of confusion.

A telephone and an answering machine at one location will also facilitate communication.

These steps allow you to establish yourself as a partnership before your program has even begun.

Family Literacy Program
700 Graham Avenue
Eau Claire, WI 54701
715-836-8474

LVA-Chippewa Valley
400 Eau Claire Street
Eau Claire, WI 54701
715-834-0222

Press releases and general news articles

Samples on the following pages depict both the start of a simpler program and the subsequent expansion to a more comprehensive program. They serve many different purposes, among them to inform, to invite, and to recognize participants.

PARENTS,

improve your own basic skills and also

READ-ALOUD

to your children and improve their chances for success.

JOIN our STORY HOUR

for parents and preschool children.

Where:
L.E. PHILLIPS MEMORIAL PUBLIC LIBRARY, Eau Claire

When:
MONDAY, JANUARY 23, 1989 • 1:00 P.M. - 2:00 P.M.
(There will be 8 Monday sessions from January 23-March 13)

To register:
Call CAROL GABLER at 834-0222
or DEBBIE LUDWIKOWSKI at 833-6349

Sponsored by
Literacy Volunteers of America-Chippewa Valley and
Chippewa Valley Technical College

Photo by Dan Reiland

Story hour

Hmong preschoolers share an activity during a story hour for them and their parents led by Carol Gabler, far right, at L.E. Phillips Memorial Public Library. Gabler is coordinator of the Literacy Volunteers of America-Chippewa Valley, which sponsors the story hour at 1 p.m. Mondays to encourage Hmong parents to read to their children. The parents also are enrolled in the LVA-Chippewa Valley tutoring program or Chippewa Valley Technical College study skills center. The Hmong story hour runs through Nov. 21. A story hour for English-speaking parents and children will begin Jan. 23. For information about either program, call 834-0222 Mondays or Tuesdays.

Special story hour for adults planned

The L.E. Phillips Memorial Public Library will hold a special story hour for adults with beginning reading skills and their preschool children from 1 to 2 p.m. Mondays, Jan. 23 through March 13.

During the story hour, parents will learn how reading to their children can be fun and helpful in their children's development. Tutors will help parents improve their own reading skills during separate sessions.

The story hour is sponsored by the Literacy Volunteers of America-Chippewa Valley, which serves new adult readers in Chippewa, Dunn, and Eau Claire counties, and the Chippewa Valley Technical College.

For more information, contact Carol Gabler at 834-0222 or Debbie Lubwikowski at 833-6349.

Family Literacy Program covering 'all the bases'

By Bob Brown
Leader-Telegram staff

September 8, 1989

> "If the learning experience is positive, I can tell you, they are going to want to come." LVA coordinator Carol Gabler

Parents and children learning together is the goal of the Family Literacy Program that will begin operation in October at the Eau Claire YMCA.

A joint venture of the YMCA, Chippewa Valley Technical College, and the Chippewa Valley affiliate of Literacy Volunteers of America, the program will help "needy parents who want to upgrade their basic skills," according to Carol Gabler, the local LVA coordinator.

The program was announced today — International Literacy Day — during a press conference at L.E. Phillips Memorial Public Library.

"If parents are able to read to their young children, going to school will be a more positive experience for the children," Gabler said.

"When parents are illiterate, children don't get the educational support they need at home. So they often repeat the negative school experiences of their parents," explained Karol Machmeier, the adult basic education and child-care services instructor at CVTC who will be coordinator of the Family Literacy Program.

The Family Literacy Program is an attempt to "break that cycle," Machmeier said.

The program is designed to serve parents who lack basic educational skills and their four-year-old children.

The parents and children will arrive at the YMCA together at 9:30 a.m. each Monday, Wednesday, and Friday. Their instruction will last until 2:30 p.m.

While the four-year-olds are participating in the YMCA's preschool program, and younger siblings are attending the YMCA child-care center, the parents will attend classes in the Masonic Temple building next door. The instructor is Dave Godlewski, an adult basic education instructor at CVTC.

Parents will receive instruction in basic reading, writing and math skills, with assistance in computer literacy, career planning, and job seeking skills. They may earn high school credits or a General Equivalency Diploma. Individualized reading instruction is available from LVA tutors.

An hour each day will be devoted to lessons in parenting skills, covering such issues as child development and guidance, stress management, nutrition and how to interact positively with children.

"Parents will also spend two hours each week assisting in the preschool program, where they can apply what they've learned in the parenting sessions," Machmeier said.

"Hopefully these skills will carry over to the home setting. Watching their children learn and succeed in the preschool program will allow parents to appreciate the potential of their children," Machmeier said.

"It's a whole new atmosphere from what they have at home," she added. "I think the parents are really going to enjoy that time with the kids."

The children's program will involve the "High Scope Curriculum," developed in Michigan for children who need stimulation and enrichment before entering a regular school setting.

"The program places emphasis on language development. It fosters independence and creativity by allowing children to choose and direct many activities," Machmeier said. The children will also receive swimming and exercise lessons.

"Having the program at the YMCA will make it fun for families," Gabler predicted. "Many of these parents have had mostly negative learning experiences. If the learning experience is positive, I can tell you, they are going to want to come."

Godlewski sees the Family Literacy Program as a way for needy parents to break out of a suffocating rut. "We're looking at people who are basically trapped in their own environment," he said. "But by providing free transportation and child care, we take away the parents' excuses. We've covered all the bases."

Covering all the bases costs money, and initially the program will be limited to 14 parents and their children, most of whom will have referrals from local schools and social service agencies.

State and federal money provided by CVTC and the Eau Claire County Human Services Department for adult basic education programs will fund the start-up of the Family Literacy Program. But Gabler and Machmeier hope to receive a $50,000 grant through the federal Even Start program to expand services.

Jack O'Connell, adult basic education coordinator at CVTC, praised the dual approach of the new program.

"We in education are pleased to be working at both ends of the problem," he said, "reaching the parent and the child."

LVA
Stars in
Literacy

On February 2nd, Shane presented his mom, Cathy, with a star representing her hard work in the family literacy program.

This program is designed to teach parents basic reading, writing and career skills while their preschool children are participating in educational experiences of their own. The goal is to break the intergenerational cycle of illiteracy by creating solid role models for their children.

If you or someone you know would like more information about available help, call 834-0222.

Letters to parents

The following is a sample letter sent out to parents of Head Start children. This could be adapted to other preschool programs as well.

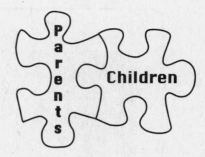

Head Start parents:

Head Start now offers a program for parents and children to learn together during the school year.

In the **Family Literacy Program**, you will have an opportunity to go to school to improve the basic skills needed to find a job or get a better one. You might choose to pursue a specific trade, or perhaps complete the requirements for a high school equivalency diploma. While you are in class, your child will attend preschool. Special time is provided for you to participate in your child's classroom. There are parenting classes available in the areas that interest you.

Please check any line that may apply to you:

_____ I am interested in working towards completing the GED tests.

_____ I would like to improve my reading, writing, math, and computer skills.

_____ I am unsure at this time and would like more information or the opportunity to visit such a program.

Name _____ Phone _____

Address _____

Child's name _____

If you checked any line, please return this form with you child's Head Start application. You will receive more information later.

> Note: This is only an interest sheet. You are not enrolling or under any obligation at this time.

This letter is a sample of one you might
send out to parents who have shown
interest in the program.

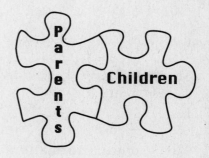

Family Literacy Program

Dear Parent and Family,

You have expressed interest in the Family Literacy Program.

We are offering two programs that will help parents continue their education while their children are in school. Child care is available.

Please read more about the programs in the enclosed brochure. For qualified families, this is a <u>free</u> opportunity, made possible by the following groups working together:

> Literacy Volunteers of America-Chippewa Valley
> Chippewa Valley Technical College
> Eau Claire Area School District
> Eau Claire County Human Services
> YMCA

I will be starting enrollment soon and will be contacting you to see if one of these programs may work for your family.

If you have moved recently or do not have a telephone, please call me at 836-8474 so we can talk more and I can answer any questions. We can only enroll about forty families, so space is limited.

Sincerely,

Family Literacy Program Lead Instructor

Sample adult learning plan
to be shared with a tutor

Student: Mary
Tutor: Ann
Date:

Background information:

During the intake interview Mary indicated her desire to eventually get her G.E.D. She is concerned about her writing skills and feels that she does not know how to study for subjects such as social studies and science.

These areas of need were confirmed by the Test of Adult Basic Education (TABE) and the Degrees of Reading Power assessment, as well as a sample of Mary's writing. (Writing sample has been included.)

Mary likes to read to her son and wants to know how to help him develop his own skills. She also reports that the letters seem "blurred" when she tries to read at night.

Initial goals:

Improve reading skills: vocabulary, comprehension
Improve writing skills: parts of speech, sentence structure, mechanics, spelling
Improve study skills
Read to child: 10 minutes, 3 times per week
Have eyes examined: within 2 months

Suggested materials and ideas for lessons:

Reading: *Reading Skills for Adults* (Steck-Vaughn, Austin, TX 1992)
Strategies for Success: Pre-GED Social Studies (Steck-Vaughn, ibid.)

Try oral reading: student to tutor, tutor to student.
Create a vocabulary notebook: new words, synonyms, antonyms, homonyms, homographs, prefixes, suffixes.
Use computer programs to develop vocabulary and increase comprehension. (See our computer coordinator if Mary is interested.)

Writing: *Connections, Life Skills and Writing* (Steck-Vaughn, Austin, TX 1992)

Work on writing skills.
Use the writing process approach we learned in tutor training.
Write together in class. Share what you each have written.

Don't worry about polishing each piece. When you are enthusiastic about a piece, I encourage you both to write more at home. A Franklin Speller [electronic spelling machine] might be a good tool for Mary to use when writing. It would help her with spelling and eliminate some of the frustration.

Study skills: *Ready, Set, Study!* (Contemporary, Chicago, IL 1990)

Helping Mary realize she has the ability to be successful in school is a priority this semester. Her social worker indicated she is very reliable and attendance should not be a problem.

Comments:

It is important for you to discuss with Mary how you will spend your 90 minutes together. I might suggest 15 minutes reading, 30 minutes working on a particular topic, 30 minutes writing, and 15 minutes reviewing.

It would be helpful if you and she could go to the public library after class sometimes and pick out children's books. Mark on your calendars when books must be returned. Introduce Mary to the children's librarians. They are happy to help parents who feel unsure about choosing books. Encourage Mary and her son to take part in the children's programs at the library. Since she drives, this should be a fun activity.

Please feel free to call if you have questions. Thank you.

Writing sample at intake:

My son Jon is three and one halve.

He relly likes books that arn't to long but I'm not allways sure what to read to him to help so he'll do good in school.

We like to go visit at Grandmas on the weekend.

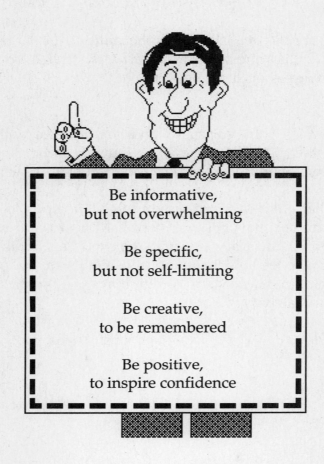

Be informative,
but not overwhelming

Be specific,
but not self-limiting

Be creative,
to be remembered

Be positive,
to inspire confidence

Appendix: Section 3
Forms to get you started

Forms listed in order of appearance:

Record keeping A - F

Program initial intake form

Authorization and release form

Adult attendance record

Adult attendance and behavior policy

Child care policy

Child field trip permission form

Assessment forms for varied purposes G - K

Checklist for comprehensive programs

Evaluation of an existing program or key component

Parent program satisfaction survey

Parent assessment of instructional quality

Tutor evaluation of tutor training

Assessment and evaluation in adult education L - N

Adult student progress report

Adult conference evaluation

Tutoring log

Assessment and evaluation in early childhood education   O - P

Child observation developmental checklist

Observation of children's behavior

Assessment and evaluation in parent education   Q - U

Personal growth and employability survey

Parenting interest survey

Parenting challenges survey

Parenting goals for discipline

End of the year evaluation: Parenting and employability

Assessment and evaluation in parent-child interaction   V - W

Report of parent / child interaction time

Evaluation of parent's oral reading

These forms were designed by the family literacy staff and regular staff
of Literacy Volunteers of America-Chippewa Valley.
They have been adapted to suit the purposes of this manual.

Purpose of Section 3:

This section presents many of the informal assessment forms used in our program. *
The program also uses observation, conference, interview, participant product, and
portfolio as assessment means. Standardized testing is important in the adult and early
childhood education program components; repeated completion of the Child Observation
Form (COR) aids assessment of the progress made by children involved in the program.
These multiple means are regarded as essential to the gathering of information important
to the evaluative judgements made for the well-being of the program and its participants.

* New forms to serve additional purposes are developed as needed.

Forms for record keeping
On page 61 there is a chart listing "Important information to document."
Some of the forms in this section help us gather and maintain those kinds of information.
Forms A - F are primarily used to:
• obtain information • state expectations • obtain permission

You may copy the forms provided in this manual.

Family Literacy Program

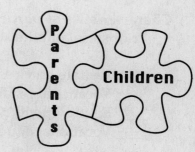

Initial Intake Form

General information:

Student name _____ Soc. Sec. no. _____

Address _____ Telephone no. _____

State & Zip _____ Date _____

Area school _____ School phone no. _____

Case manager _____ JOBS or JTPA? Yes _____ No _____

Educational needs:

_____ G.E.D. _____ Math _____ Computers _____ Upgrade skills

_____ Writing _____ Reading _____ Parenting _____ Employability

Highest school year completed _____ School attended_____

Test results available? Yes _____ No _____ From where?_____

Employment _____When last? _____

Placement:

Days available: M _____ T _____ W _____ Th _____ F _____

Transportation: Car _____ School bus _____ City bus _____

Date arranged _____ Starting date _____ Ending date _____

Site _____ Tutor needed? Yes _____ No _____

Tutor name _____ Date assigned _____

Tutor phone number _____

A

Characteristics of participant:
Prior social or educational services received:

____ Welfare services   ____ Adult basic education (0-4)
____ Vocational rehabilitation   ____ Adult basic education (5-8)
____ Employment training   ____ Adult secondary education (9-12)
____ Vocational education   ____ English as a Second Language

Social/educational services currently participating in:

____ Welfare service   ____ Vocational education
____ Employment training   ____ Vocational rehabilitation
____ Other

Possible future goals: _____

_____

Family structure:
____ Couple with children   ____ Single parent with children
____ Foster parents   ____ Grandparents

Number of adult household members (18+) _____
Number of children (0-7) _____   Number of children (8-18) _____

Financial support for the family:
Income: ____ $5,000-10,000 ____ $10,000-15,000 ____ Over $15,000

Family assistance programs: _____

_____

_____

Children:

Name	Age	School
1._____	_____	_____
2._____	_____	_____
3._____	_____	_____
4._____	_____	_____

A

Educational status of children:

	Head Start	Preschool	Spec Ed*	Kgarten	None	Other
Child #1 Gender ____ Birthdate _____						
Previous educ.						
Current educ.						
Child #2 Gender ____ Birthdate _____						
Previous educ.						
Current educ.						
Child #3 Gender ____ Birthdate _____						
Previous educ.						
Current educ.						
Child #4 Gender ____ Birthdate _____						
Previous educ.						
Current educ.						

*Early intervention/early childhood special education

Comments:

_____

_____

_____

_____

_____

A

Family Literacy Program
Authorization and Release Form

Student name _____ Soc. Sec. no. _____

Address _____ Telephone no. _____

State & Zip _____ Date_____

Examine records:
I authorize and permit the _____family literacy staff to examine my past records or share my current records for the express purpose of developing my education plan.

I hereby give my permission to the staff named above to request or share the following information:
____ medical information   ____ educational records   ____ work history
____ assessment/training information   ____ other _____

This information may be released to the following for educational and employment planning purposes: _____ adult education staff   _____ counseling services
_____ child care providers   _____ school district
_____ department of social services

Written materials:
I authorize and permit the family literacy staff named above to reprint materials I have written. I give my permission for these materials to be used in tutor-training workshops, the newsletter, and any other use deemed helpful to promote the program. Yes ____ No ____

Photos:
I authorize and permit the family literacy staff named above to use my photograph and/or my child's photograph in publications or any other use deemed helpful to promote the program. Yes ____ No ____

Permission is given for the following period of time:_____ to _____
I understand the meaning of the above authorizations.

Student's signature _____ Date _____

Staff member _____ Title _____
unconditional permission to copy

B

Family Literacy Program

Adult Attendance Record

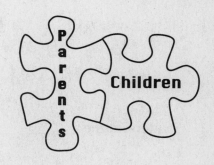

Date _____

Name	AM/In	AM/Out	PM/In	PM/Out	ABE	PAR	PAC

ABE: Adult Basic Education　　　PAR: Parent education　　　PAC: Parent/child interaction time

C

Family Literacy Program

Adult Attendance and Behavior Policy

Student name _____ Telephone no._____

Attendance policy:

1. Regular attendance is expected of all students enrolled in Family Literacy.
2. Outside appointments not related to Family Literacy are to be scheduled outside of class time.
3. Students are to arrive for class on time and may not leave early unless arrangements are made with the instructor.
4. Attendance is reported to agencies involved as requested.
5. Students must call Family Literacy to report excused absences.

Behavior policy:

1. Smoking is allowed only in designated areas, using proper ash trays.
2. Food and beverages are allowed in the classroom only when instructor permits them.
3. No visitors or guests may attend without prior arrangement.
4. Showing respect for property and other students is required.
5. The possession or use of a controlled substance (drugs or alcohol) will result in suspension or other disciplinary action.

A student may be dropped from the program for:

1. Distracting behavior that interferes with teaching.
2. Disruptive behavior toward other students.
3. Profane/abusive language.
4. Uncooperative/disrespectful behavior.
5. Not progressing in class or sleeping in class.
6. Too many absences, excused or unexcused.

I have read the above policies and understand what is expected of me.

Student signature _____ Date _____

Instructor _____

unconditional permission to copy

D

Family Literacy Program

Child Care Policy

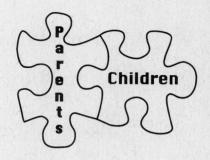

Family literacy child care <u>may</u> be used for:

1. family literacy program hours.

2. appointments which are directly related to family literacy.
    * Testing appointment for G.E.D.
    * Tours through adult education programs
    * Registration at adult education program

3. appointments through the social services which cannot be scheduled for non-class time.

4. parent participation in the classroom of an older sibling.

Family literacy child care <u>may</u> <u>not</u> be used for:

1. doctor or dental appointments.

2. rental or housing problems.

3. appointments which may be scheduled during non-class time days or hours.

4. any outside appointment not related to family literacy or human services employment program.

The child care staff must know where you are at all times.

I have read and understood the child care policy stated above.

Student's signature _____ Date _____
unconditional permission to copy

E

Family Literacy Program

Field Trip Permission Form

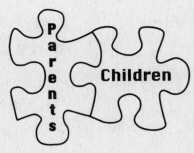

Student name _____

Address _____ Telephone no. _____

State & Zip _____ Emergency contact _____

My child, _____, has my permission

to visit _____

on this date _____ with the family literacy staff.

I give my permission for my child to ride in a private automobile to go on this

field trip. I will not hold _____ or any family

literacy partners responsible for any accident or injury that occurs to my child.

I understand that if I drive my own car and take my own child and other

passengers, I must have liability insurance and a valid driver's license. My driver's

license number is _____. I take full responsibility for any

accident, property damage or personal injury that occurs to me.

I understand that _____ and the family literacy

partners do not have automobile insurance to cover injuries and damage.

Signature of parent: _____

Date signed: _____

unconditional permission to copy

F

Assessment forms for various purposes

Many decisions must be made in the planning, implementation, and assessment of a family literacy program. The instruments presented in this section are useful in making decisions regarding program components, based on the perceived value and quality of the offerings.

Forms G - K are used to:

- Assess program comprehensiveness
- Conduct a program evaluation
- Determine parent satisfaction with their own growth
- Determine parent perception of program quality
- Determine tutors' evaluation of their training program

Checklist for Comprehensive Family Literacy Programs

Directions: This checklist of elements important to a comprehensive family literacy program is based on the material presented in this book. To determine the status of your existing program, circle the appropriate number opposite each item, according to the following key:

> #1 = This **exists** in our program.
> #2 = This **is needed** in our program.
> #3 = This **will not be included** in our program.

I.   Goal statements:
   1.   outcomes sought through overall program 1   2   3
   2.   outcomes sought through each key component 1   2   3

II.   Key components:
   3.   education for the adult 1   2   3
   4.   education for the preschool child 1   2   3
   5.   parent education 1   2   3
   6.   parent-child interaction 1   2   3

III. Partners in a comprehensive program:
   7.   literacy program 1   2   3
   8.   institutions for higher education 1   2   3
   9.   sibling childcare providers 1   2   3
   10.   local educational programs 1   2   3
   11.   library 1   2   3
   12.   social services 1   2   3
   13.   funding agencies 1   2   3

IV.   Essential activities:
   14.   partner involvement 1   2   3
   15.   tutor training 1   2   3
   16.   publicity 1   2   3
   17.   family recruitment 1   2   3
   18.   ongoing family involvement (home visits) 1   2   3
   19.   seeking funding 1   2   3
   20.   English as a Second Language 1   2   3

V.   Organization:
   21.   governing body 1   2   3
   22.   coordination committee 1   2   3
   23.   coordinator 1   2   3
   24.   needed staff 1   2   3
   25.   funding plan 1   2   3

VI.   Assessment and evaluation:
   26.   procedures for program planning 1   2   3
   27.   procedures for program implementation 1   2   3
   28.   procedures to determine program effectiveness 1   2   3

Evaluation of an existing program or key component

Use this procedure to ensure alignment of the assessment and evaluation processes with your decision-making needs. Answer all items before beginning the process.

1. List those who will make decisions about the programs: (individuals and/or groups)

2. List the decisions that need to be made:

3. List the options to be considered for each decision to be made:

4. Describe the information/data needs as dictated by the decisions and options:

5. Describe the information-gathering procedures/instruments appropriate for gathering the needed information/data.

6. Describe the information/data gathering procedure, i.e. by whom? when? where? how?

7. Describe the information/data analysis procedure, i.e. how? by whom? when?

8. Describe the procedures for providing results to the decision-maker, i.e. how? when? by whom?

H

Parent Program Satisfaction Survey

Purpose: To determine how satisfied you are with the growth you made (or your child made) in various phases of the Family Literacy Program.

Directions: For each item listed below, indicate how satisfied you are with the growth you made (or your child made) by circling the appropriate number from the following key:

3 = very satisfied   **2 = satisfied**   **1 = not satisfied**

Adult Basic Education (ABE): My growth in

1. mathematics skills 3 2 1
2. reading skills 3 2 1
3. writing skills 3 2 1
4. computer skills 3 2 1
5. study skills 3 2 1
6. ability to use time well 3 2 1
7. enjoyment of reading 3 2 1
8. ability to do a job search 3 2 1
9. preparation for a job 3 2 1

Early childhood education: My child's growth in

10. the ability to get along with others 3 2 1
11. self-esteem 3 2 1
12. physical coordination 3 2 1
13. positive feelings about school 3 2 1
14. preparation for school (pre-reading, pre-writing)......................... 3 2 1

Parenting: My growth in

15. understanding my child's growth and development 3 2 1
16. learning new ways to guide my child's behavior 3 2 1
17. learning to communicate more positively with my child 3 2 1
18. selecting and reading good books to my child 3 2 1
19. gaining new information from speakers in the community 3 2 1
20. improving my family's health 3 2 1

Parent-child interaction activities: (Through activities such as PACT time, Parent Pacs, volunteering in the children's room, RIF, and home visits) My growth in

21. better understanding how my child learns 3 2 1
22. feeling more comfortable in my child's classroom 3 2 1
23. being able to learn new things to do together 3 2 1
24. being able to have fun together 3 2 1

I

Services: If you used any or all of the following services, indicate your feelings according to the following key. If you did not use service, circle #0.

Key: 3 = YES 2 = NO 1 = Uncertain 0 = Service not used

25. The transportation services helped me get to school 3 2 1 0
26. The sibling childcare service helped my family 3 2 1 0
27. The social worker helped me succeed in school 3 2 1 0
28. My child benefited from referrals to special services 3 2 1 0
29. The literacy tutor helped me 3 2 1 0

In general: Indicate your feeling about each statement by circling

3 = YES **2 = NO** **1 = Uncertain**

30. The program improved my self-esteem 3 2 1
31. The program helped my child's development 3 2 1
32. The program helped our family life 3 2 1
33. My future looks better to me now than it did before
participating in the program 3 2 1

Final direction: For any item that you responded "not satisfied" on page one, please write the number below and explain what you think should have been done in the Family Literacy Program to help you accomplish more. Thank you!

<u>Number</u> <u>Explanation</u>

Whooley 1995

I

Parent Assessment of Instructional Quality

Purpose: To determine how you feel about the quality of the instruction that was provided your child and you in the Family Literacy Program.

Directions: Using the key below, circle the number that best describes how you feel about the quality of instruction that was provided with reference to each item listed below.

> 5 = excellent
> 4 = good
> 3 = acceptable
> 2 = poor
> 1 = very poor

I. Adult Basic Education: The quality of instruction provided to develop my abilities in

A. mathematics	5	4	3	2	1
B. reading	5	4	3	2	1
C. writing	5	4	3	2	1
D. computer use	5	4	3	2	1
E. preparing for employment	5	4	3	2	1

II. Parenting: The quality of instruction provided to help me understand

F. child growth and development	5	4	3	2	1
G. how to guide children's behavior	5	4	3	2	1
H. how to provide a home environment supportive of learning	5	4	3	2	1
I. how to improve family health and fitness	5	4	3	2	1

III. Early childhood education: The quality of instruction provided to improve my child's

J. emotional well-being	5	4	3	2	1
K. social well-being	5	4	3	2	1
L. physical well-being	5	4	3	2	1
M. preparation for formal schooling (pre-reading, pre-writing)	5	4	3	2	1

IV. Parent-child interaction: The quality of the learning opportunities provided to:

N. improve parent-child relationships	5	4	3	2	1
O. promote interaction activities	5	4	3	2	1

We are seeking helpful comments. If you comment on any item, please indicate the letter of the item you are discussing. Please write comments on the back of this page. Thank you.

Whooley 1995

J

Evaluation of Tutor Training

Part One

Purpose: To obtain tutor assessment of the content of tutor training sessions.

Directions: Circle the response indicating how extensive you feel the coverage of each content area should be.

Treatment of this topic should be:
- **A. maintained as is**
- **B. increased**
- **C. decreased**
- **D. maintained with modifications***

*We invite comments. Please place the topic number in front of the comment.

1. The qualities and characteristics of adult students .... A B C D
2. The collaborative process in tutoring and the role of an effective tutor .... A B C D
3. Characteristics of an effective tutor .... A B C D
4. Perspectives on the reading process .... A B C D
5. Reading for comprehension .... A B C D
6. Relationship of thought, oral language, and written communication .... A B C D
7. Techniques and strategies for working with adult students:
    a. language experience .... A B C D
    b. sight words .... A B C D
    c. phonics .... A B C D
    d. word patterns .... A B C D
8. Real-life materials .... A B C D
9. The impact of culture on learning a second language .... A B C D
10. Techniques for teaching ESL students .... A B C D
11. English survival skills for ESL students .... A B C D
12. Initiating the writing process with a student .... A B C D
13. Steps in the writing process .... A B C D
14. Relationship of assessment, goal analysis, and lesson planning A B C D
15. Lesson planning .... A B C D
16. Goal-setting and student needs .... A B C D
17. Assessment of student progress, short term and long term ...... A B C D

Comments:

Evaluation of Tutor Training

Part Two
Directions: Please answer these questions.

1. What, if any, additional topics would you like to see included in this program?

2. What topics or activities were the most useful to you in your preparation to become a tutor?

3. If you are working (or have worked) with an ESL student, please respond to the following questions:

   Was the training you received adequate preparation for tutoring an ESL student?

   Would you attend additional ESL training sessions if offered? _____

Overall rating

1. For tutoring adult students, the program provided me: (Check one)
   ____ excellent preparation.
   ____ adequate preparation.
   ____ minimal preparation.
   ____ less than minimal preparation.

2. Overall, I rate the tutor training program: (Check one)
   ____ excellent
   ____ good
   ____ adequate
   ____ poor
   ____ of no value

Thank you for your contributions to this program!

K

Forms for assessing a key component:
adult education

The primary goals for adult education are basic education and job preparation. Each parent pursues those goals through an individualized learning plan. Information regarding the learners' progress towards additional goals and/or the modification of goals is important. Tutors that we train assist the adults. It is important to assess initial tutoring sessions and to maintain ongoing contact.

Forms L - N are used to:

- Determine student/tutor perception of progress toward goals
- Assess student accomplishments, concerns, and goals
- Follow tutors into their initial tutoring experiences

For a list of standardized tests currently available in adult education, contact:

- Chapter 1 Technical Assistance Center
  Region C/Test Information Center
  1979 Lakeside Parkway, Suite 400
  Tucker, GA 30084
  (800) 241-3865

Ask for:
- Selected Academic Skills Tests for Adults
- Selected Educational Tests for Speakers of Languages Other than English

Adult Student Progress Report

Purpose: The purpose of this report is to document student progress for the semester.
Directions: The interviewer should discuss the form with the student and/or tutor and record the information. The interviewer will complete only those sections which apply to the individual.

Student _____ Tutor _____

Date _____ Semester (please circle):   fall   winter   summer

Interviewer _____

---

1. Reading Goals

List reading goals student worked on this
semester, in order of importance to student.

	No progress toward goal	Some progress toward goal	Attained goal
a. _____	[ ]	[ ]	[ ]
b. _____	[ ]	[ ]	[ ]
c. _____	[ ]	[ ]	[ ]
d. _____	[ ]	[ ]	[ ]

What assessment procedures were used?

_____

_____

2. Writing Goals

List writing goals student worked on, in order of importance to student.

(checks, notes, memos, forms, applications, letters,
reports, stories, poems, other)

	No progress toward goal	Some progress toward goal	Attained goal
a. _____	[ ]	[ ]	[ ]
b. _____	[ ]	[ ]	[ ]
c. _____	[ ]	[ ]	[ ]
d. _____	[ ]	[ ]	[ ]

What assessment procedures were used?

_____

_____

3. **Life Goals**
   List life goals student worked on, in order of importance to student.

   (GED, citizenship, computer skills, job-related skills, driver's license, regular attendance, improved self-esteem, other)

	No progress toward goal	Some progress toward goal	Attained goal
a. _____	[ ]	[ ]	[ ]
b. _____	[ ]	[ ]	[ ]
c. _____	[ ]	[ ]	[ ]
d. _____	[ ]	[ ]	[ ]

   What assessment procedures were used?

   _____

   _____

4. **Understanding spoken English**   (For ESL students only)
   List goals student worked on for understanding spoken English, in order of importance to student.

   (related to general conversation, telephone skills, jobs, medical, business, school, safety, and transportation)

	No progress toward goal	Some progress toward goal	Attained goal
a. _____	[ ]	[ ]	[ ]
b. _____	[ ]	[ ]	[ ]
c. _____	[ ]	[ ]	[ ]
d. _____	[ ]	[ ]	[ ]

   What assessment procedures were used?

   _____

   _____

5. **Speaking understandable English**   (For ESL students only)
   List goals student worked on for speaking understandable English, in order of importance to student.

   (related to general conversation, telephone skills, jobs, medical, business, school, safety, and transportation)

	No progress toward goal	Some progress toward goal	Attained goal
a. _____	[ ]	[ ]	[ ]
b. _____	[ ]	[ ]	[ ]
c. _____	[ ]	[ ]	[ ]
d. _____	[ ]	[ ]	[ ]

   What assessment procedures were used?

   _____

Family Literacy Program

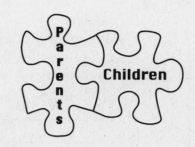

Adult Conference Evaluation: Mid-Semester and Year-End

Student name _____ Date _____

Class hours attended_____ Percentage of hours offered_____% Tutor hours _____

Entry level _____ Past testing: Date _____Test _____ Score_____

Exit level _____ Current test: Date_____Test _____ Score_____

Student accomplishments:

_____

_____

_____

Concerns:

_____

_____

_____

Future goals: _____

_____

Plans for next semester: ____ Return to family literacy   ____ Seek employment
                              ____ Attend other training   ____ Other

Student suggestions/comments: _____

_____

Conclusions: _____

_____

M

Family Literacy Program
Tutoring Log

Name of tutor _____ Name of student _____

Where will you meet? _____ When will you meet? _____

Length of tutoring sessions _____ Date _____

We are interested in supporting you as you work with your student.
Please return this form after your second session.

First session
Brief summary of session (materials and activities):

Ideas for next session:

Any problems?

Any progress?

Second session
Brief summary of session (materials and activities):

Ideas for next session:

Any problems?

Any progress?

_____ I would like you to contact me for additional help.

unconditional permission to copy

N

Forms for assessing a key component: early childhood education

The goal of early childhood education is to provide developmental experiences conducive to continuing success in education. Parent and instructor observation of child development is important to the provision of appropriate developmental experience at home and in preschool.

Forms O - P are used to:

- Help parent/instructor assess stages of a child's development
- Record observations of selected learning activities

For a list of standardized tests currently available in early childhood education, contact:

- Chapter 1 Technical Assistance Center
  Region D/4
  Overland Park, KS
  (800) 922-9031

Ask for:
- Selected Early Childhood Assessments

Family Literacy Program

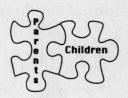

Child Observation Developmental Checklist

Child name _____   Birthdate _____

Age & date at 1st check:_____ / _____   2nd check: _____ / _____

Terms used: NU =   Not Usually
              ST =   Some of the Time
              AA =   Almost Always

Physical development:

1. _____ _____ Good general health and hygiene
(vision, hearing, weight, eating habits, manners, etc.)
2. _____ _____ Good large muscle control and coordination -- gross motor
(running, walking, jumping, climbing, throwing, etc.)
3. _____ _____ Good small muscle control and coordination -- fine motor
(drawing, printing, scissor skills)
(puzzles, shelf toys, building blocks, etc.)

Comments:

_____

_____

Speech and language development:

1. _____ _____ Speaks clearly (articulation and letter sounds)

2. _____ _____ Talks in sentences; asks, answers questions

3. _____ _____ Expresses ideas, feelings, and needs — using words

4. _____ _____ Initiates conversation during play and contributes to group time

Comments:

_____

_____

Social development:

1. _____   _____ Cooperates, shares, respects other children, and takes turns

2. _____   _____ Interacts positively with teachers and other adults

3. _____   _____ Is able to play alone or in groups

Comments:

_____

_____

Emotional development:

1. _____   _____ Likes school, seems generally happy and secure

2. _____   _____ Responds appropriately with parent in the room

3. _____   _____ Accepts limits and shows ability to control own behavior

4. _____   _____ Feels confident of own ability and shows positive self-esteem

Comments:

_____

_____

Intellectual (thinking or cognitive) development:

1. _____   _____ Shows good general knowledge and awareness of things
                        (knows name, age, animals, events, etc.)
2. _____   _____ Uses age-appropriate vocabulary

3. _____   _____ Demonstrates good understanding of concepts
                        (big, short, high, first, more, etc.)
4. _____   _____ Has age-appropriate recognition of colors, numbers, letters

Comments:

_____

School readiness skills:

1. _____ _____ Demonstrates adequate skills in independent behaviors (dressing, eating, using the toilet, clean-up)
2. _____ _____ Is motivated to try and eager to learn new things

3. _____ _____ Can concentrate, stay on task, complete an activity

4. _____ _____ Listens, comprehends, and follows directions

5. _____ _____ Shows some problem-solving abilities (handles frustration, tries new ideas, asks for help)
6. _____ _____ Enjoys books, stories, reading and writing activities

Comments:

_____

_____

Areas child plays in at school on regular basis:

1. _____ _____ Art activities

2. _____ _____ Quiet activities (puzzles, shelf games)

3. _____ _____ Building (blocks, Legos, sand)

4. _____ _____ Books

5. _____ _____ Family (kitchen, dress-up, pretend)

Comments:

_____

_____

_____

Observation of Children's Behavior

Period of observation: From (mon./yr.) _____ to (mon./yr.) _____

Checklist code: **N** = Never **S** = Sometimes **AA** = Almost Always

Behavior:	1* ..books..			2* ...writing..			3* ...labeling..			4* ...new words..			5* ...review..		
Child's name:	N	S	AA	N	S	AA	N	S	AA	N	S	AA	N	S	AA

1*   Looks at books in free time
2*   Uses writing center in free time
3*   Participates in labeling activities
4*   Uses new words
5*   Is able to plan, do, & review activities

You may copy this page.

Forms for assessing a key component:
parent education

The goal for parent education is to assist parents in developing the behavior patterns and skills necessary to function effectively as parents and providers. The curriculum provided to achieve this goal is enhanced by asking parents what they perceive to be their educational needs.

Forms Q - U are used to:

- Determine parent concerns affecting personal growth and employability
- Identify areas of parent interest
- Assess parent disciplinary strengths and weaknesses
- Survey parent opinions on parenting component

Personal Growth and Employability Interest Survey

This is a list of topics helpful to adults who are working to build their personal, educational, and employability skills. <u>Please check those that are of most interest to you.</u>

_____ Building self-esteem
       Attitude
       Motivation
       Assertiveness
       Communication

_____ Emergency food, housing, clothing

_____ Depression/mental health issues

_____ Managing anger

_____ Dieting/personal appearance

_____ Exercise/physical fitness

_____ Family planning/birth control

_____ Alcohol/drug abuse

_____ Resolving conflict/problems

_____ Adult relationships

_____ Using community resources

_____ Support group information

_____ WIC (Women, Infants, Children)

_____ PIC (Private Industry Council)

_____ DVR (Div. Vocational Rehab.)

_____ Budget/stretching dollars

_____ Consumer awareness
Smart buying
Handling complaints, etc.

_____ Driver's license

_____ Understanding charts, labels, billing systems

_____ Understanding forms, legal documents

_____ Working with social services

_____ Career planning

_____ Finding a job
       Reading ads
       Filling out applications
       Resume writing
       Interviewing skills

_____ What employers look for

_____ How to succeed in college, technical training programs

_____ Other topics of interest:

_____

_____

Q

Parenting Interest Survey

The following list includes many topics found to be of interest to parents.
<u>Please check the ones you would like to learn more about.</u>

_____ Family nutrition

_____ Dental/health concerns

_____ Home safety and sanitation

_____ First aid/CPR

_____ Finding good childcare

_____ Ways to strengthen families

_____ Managing children's behavior

_____ Sibling rivalry

_____ Living with adolescents

_____ Violence and aggression in children

_____ Ages and stages of development

_____ Understanding children's play

_____ "Readiness for school"

_____ Working with teachers/schools

_____ Helping children learn

_____ Learning disabilities

_____ Handicapped children

_____ Improved reading aloud skills

_____ Choosing good children's books

_____ Choosing good children's toys

_____ Television and children

_____ At-home activities for children

_____ Stepparenting issues

_____ Single parent issues:
Custody
Child support
Visitation, etc.

_____ Talking to children about:
Divorce
Sex
Death and dying
Fears and feelings

_____ Child abuse and neglect

_____ Alcoholism's effect of children

_____ Other areas of interest

_____

_____

unconditional permission to copy

R

Parenting Challenges Survey

This is a list of some of the most common problems parents have when managing children's behavior. <u>Check those that concern you the most.</u>

_____ Poor eating habits

    _____ Overeating

    _____ Not eating

    _____ Playing with food

_____ Poor sleep habits

    _____ Getting up in the night

    _____ Toileting accidents

_____ Aggressive behavior

    _____ Talking back

    _____ Demanding own way

    _____ Name-calling

    _____ Destroying property

    _____ Throwing temper tantrums

_____ Dependent behavior

    _____ Being possessive

    _____ Clinging to parents

    _____ Dawdling

    _____ Whining

_____ Uncooperative behavior

    _____ Refusing to clean up

    _____ Not following directions

_____ Problems in public

    _____ Interacting with strangers

    _____ Wandering away

    _____ Getting into things

    _____ Taking things

_____Traveling problems

    _____ Resisting car seats

_____ List other areas of concern:

_____

_____

_____

S

Family Literacy Program

Parenting Goals for Discipline

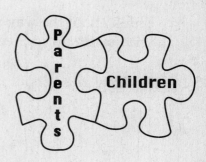

Parent's name _____ Date _____

Child's name _____ Age (years and months) _____

Purpose: Questions 1-4 will help you develop a plan to strengthen the good behaviors in your child and change the undesirable ones. Questions 5-8 will help you understand and improve your methods of discipline.

1. Write down the **good (positive) behaviors** you usually see in this child. (List as many as you can.)

2. Write down the **misbehaviors** you see in this child that often create problems.

3. Select the two behaviors from #1 above that you most want your child to continue to practice. Write them on the spaces below.

    _____

    _____

4. Select the two misbehaviors from #2 above that you most want your child to change. Write them down on the spaces below.

    _____

    _____

5. Think about the way you discipline your child. Complete the following statement with **methods** you feel are **positive**.

   I feel good about the way I:

6. Sometimes we react to children's misbehavior in **negative** ways. Complete the following statement with discipline methods that concern you.

   I am concerned about the way I:

7. Choose the two methods from #5 above that you most want to **continue** and list them below.

   _____

   _____

8. Choose the two methods from #6 above that you most want to **change**.

   _____

   _____

Remember to praise your child's positive behaviors.

Make it your goal to react to the negative behaviors using discipline methods that you have listed as positive.

T

Family Literacy Program

End of the year survey: Parenting and employability

Parent's name _____   Date _____

1.   My child is in:

_____ Headstart   _____ Preschool

_____ Kindergarten   _____ Other

2.   I feel this program has helped my child learn and develop:

_____ Not at all   _____ Somewhat   _____ Greatly

Examples of gains I have seen:

_____

_____

_____

3.   I feel the parenting component of this program has benefited me:

_____ Not at all   _____ Somewhat   _____ Greatly

Example of something I have learned or am now doing differently as a parent:

_____

_____

_____

4.   Parenting activities that I liked (please check):

_____ Take-home packets _____ Group discussions   _____ Hand-outs

_____ Speakers   _____ Whole group activities _____ PACT time

_____ Helping in my child's classroom   _____ Information from instructor

U

5. I feel participating in the above activities has helped me grow personally and professionally:

_____ Not at all   _____ Somewhat   _____ Greatly

Example of something I have learned:

_____

_____

_____

6. Personal growth/employability activities that I liked (please check):

_____ Speakers   _____ Group discussions   _____ Hand-outs

7. Ways I feel the family literacy program could be improved:

_____

_____

_____

8. My comments about the family literacy program overall:

_____

_____

_____

Forms for assessing a key component: parent-child interaction

The goal in parent-child interaction is to provide opportunities for parents and their children to learn together. Helping parents interact more effectively with their children involves literacy skills and the ability to analyze the interactions that occur.

Forms V - W are used to:

- Determine parent perceptions of interaction opportunities
- Assess parent literacy skills

Family Literacy Program

Report of Parent-Child Interaction Time

Parent's name _____ Date _____ Time _____

Child's name _____

What did you do in your child's classroom today?

_____

_____

_____

_____

What did your child do?

_____

_____

_____

What did you do together?

_____

_____

_____

How do you feel about the time spent?   Why?

_____

_____

_____

unconditional permission to copy

Evaluation of Parent's Oral Reading

Parent's name _____   Child's name _____

Tutor _____

Story _____   Date _____

(To be completed by tutor, peer partner, or other observer.)

Mark one box for each skill listed.

Skill	Needs practice	Able to complete the task	Shows competence
1. Pronounces all words in story correctly			
2. Reads with expression and inflection			
3. Asks appropriate questions of child			
4. Responds with understanding to child's comments and questions			

Does the parent seem comfortable reading to the child?

Are there any other relevant observations?

Appendix: Section 4
Resource lists and bibliography

Index to resource lists

Valuable resources for family literacy programs

Organizations that promote family literacy

Even Start Program

Compensatory Education Program
Office of Elementary and Secondary Education
U.S. Department of Education
400 Maryland Avenue, SW
Washington, DC 20202-6132   (202) 401-1692

Contact your state department of education.

Services offered: Funding for programs which integrate early childhood
                       education and adult education based on collaboration of
                       community resources

Literacy Volunteers of America

5795 Widewaters Parkway
Syracuse, NY 13214   (315) 445-8000

Services offered: Assistance for literacy providers
                       Instructional and training materials
                       Volunteer program
                       Management materials: 50/50 Training,
                            Verse Computer Management System
                       Reading with Children program
                       Annual conference

National Center for Family Literacy

Waterfront Plaza, Suite 200
325 West Main Street
Louisville, KY 40202-4251   (502) 584-1133

Services offered: Pre-implementation seminars for administrators and
                       policymakers
                       Implementation training for teachers and other program
                            staff
                       Publications and videotapes for awareness, training,
                            program development, curriculum building, and
                            evaluation
                       National evaluation, validation, and dissemination of
                            effective programs and promising practices
                       Quarterly newsletter
                       Annual conference

Laubach Literacy Action

1320 Jamesville Avenue
P.O. Box 131
Syracuse, NY 13210   (315) 422-9121

Services offered: Assistance for literacy providers
                      Instructional and training materials
                      Volunteer program management materials
                      Annual conference

National Institute for Literacy

800 Connecticut Avenue NW, Suite 200
Washington, DC 20006   (202) 632-1500

Origin: Independent federal agency funded though offices of
                      Secretary of Education, Secretary of Labor, and
                      Secretary of Health and Human Services

Services offered: Coordination and enhancement of literacy efforts at all
                      levels
                      Collaboration with Congress on literacy initiatives
                      Grant funding
                      Informational retrieval systems to link resources and
                      disseminate research

International Reading Association

800 Barksdale Road
P.O. Box 8139
Newark, DE 19714-8139   (302) 731-1600, ext. 215

Services offered: Clearinghouse for the dissemination of reading research
                      through conferences, journals, and other publications

Reading Is Fundamental (RIF), Inc.

Programs Division
600 Maryland Avenue, SW
Suite 500
Washington, DC 20024   (202) 287-3220

Services offered: Reading motivation program that works with children
                      and families, providing free materials and special
                      programs for at-risk families

Barbara Bush Foundation for Family Literacy
1002 Wisconsin Avenue, NW
Washington, DC 20007   (202) 338-2006

Services offered: Funding source for development of family literacy prgrams
Support for training and professional development of
teachers

American Library Association (ALA)
Office for Library Outreach Services
50 East Huron Street
Chicago, IL 60601   (312) 944-6780

Institute for the Study of Adult Literacy
Pennsylvania State University
204 Calder Way, Suite 209
University Park, PA 16801-4756   (814) 863-3777

Services offered: Staff development and instructional materials
Dissemination of research
Newsletter

Illinois Literacy Resource Development Center
269 West Clark Street
Champaign, IL 61820 (217) 355-6068

ERIC Clearinghouse on Adult, Career, and Vocational Education
Center on Education and Training for Employment
Ohio State University
1900 Kenny Road
Columbus, OH 43210 (614) 292-4353
(800) 848-4815

National Clearinghouse on Literacy Education
Center for Applied Linguistics
1118 22nd Street, NW
Washington, DC 20037   (202) 429-9292

Project Literacy U.S.   (PLUS)
WQED
4802 Fifth Avenue
Pittsburgh, PA   15213   (412) 622-1300

Materials helpful in program development

Adult Literacies: Intersections with Elementary and Secondary Education
    Edited by Caroline Beverstock and Anabel Newman (1991)
        Phi Delta Kappa
        Box 789
        Bloomington, IN 47402   (812) 339-1156

Community Collaborations for Family Literacy Handbook
    By Shelly Quezada & Ruth S. Nickse (1993)
        Neal-Schuman Publishers, Inc.
        100 Varick Street
        New York, NY 10013

Generation to Generation: Realizing the Promise of Family Literacy
    By Jack Brizius and Susan Foster (1993)
        National Center for Family Literacy
        High/Scope Press
        600 N. River St.
        Ypsilanti, MI 48197

Maintaining the Balance: A Guide to 50/50 Management
    By Anne DuPrey (1993)
        Literacy Volunteers of America, Inc.
        5795 Widewaters Parkway
        Syracuse, NY 13214   (315) 445-8000

Strategies for Building Collaborative Relationships and Articulated Programs
    By Judith A. Alamprese
        Paper presented at Transitions: Building Partnerships Between Literacy
        Volunteer and Adult Education Programs (1994 national conference sponsored
        by U.S. Department of Education, Washington, DC).

    Reprints available from the author: Judith Alamprese
                                                1735 Eye Street, NW, Suite 613
                                                Washington, DC   20006
                                                (202) 728-3939

Working with Families: Promising Programs to Help Parents Support Young Children's
    Learning; Executive Summary
    By Goodson, B.D., Swartz, J.P., and Millsap, M.A. (February 1991)
        Final Report for the U.S. Department of Education, Office of Planning, Budget
        and Evaluation.

Adult education resources

Adult Literacy: Contexts and Challenges
By Anabel Newman and Caroline Beverstock (1990)
International Reading Association
800 Barksdale Road
Newark, DE 19714-8139

American Association for Adult and Continuing Education (AAACE)
1112 Sixteenth Street NW, Suite 420
Washington, D.C. 20036 (202) 463-6333

Celebrate Writing, a collection of adult student writings
Put it in Print, a manual for producing a book of student writings
Published by Chippewa Valley Publishing
Literacy Volunteers of America-Chippewa Valley
400 Eau Claire St.
Eau Claire, WI 54701 (715) 834-0222
(Ordering information is on back page of this manual.)

Chapter 1 Technical Assistance Center
Region C TAC
1979 Lakeside Parkway, Suite 400
Tucker, GA 30084 (800) 241-3865

Collaboration Through Writing and Reading
By A. H. Dyson (Ed.) (1989)
National Council of Teachers of English
1111 West Kenyon Road
Urbana, IL 61801-1096

ERIC Clearinghouse on Adult, Career, and Vocational Education
Center on Education and Training for Employment
Ohio State University
1900 Kenny Road
Columbus, OH (800) 848-4815

Mosaic: Research Notes on Literacy, free newsletter
Published by Institute for the Study of Adult Literacy
College of Education, Pennsylvania State University
204 Calder Way, Suite 209
University Park, PA 16801-4756 (814) 863-3777

Early childhood education resources

Chapter 1 Technical Assistance Center
    Region D/4
    9209 West 110th Street
    Overland Park, KS 66210   (800) 922-9031

ERIC Clearinghouse on Elementary and Early Childhood Education
    University of Illinois
    805 West Pennsylvania Avenue
    Urbana, IL 61801   (217) 333-1386

National Association for the Education of Young Children
    1509 16th Street, N.W.
    Washington, DC 20036-1426   (202) 232-8777

    Brochures: #547   Developmentally Appropriate Practice in Early
                          Childhood Programs Serving Infants
                #508   Developmentally Appropriate Practice in Early
                          Childhood Programs Serving Toddlers
                #522   Good Teaching Practices for 4- and 5-Year-Olds

Telling Tales: How to produce a book of stories by parents and their children
    By Jan Goethel and LVA-CV Family Literacy Staff (1995)
        Chippewa Valley Publishing
        400 Eau Claire Street
        Eau Claire, WI 54703   (715) 834-0222
                (See ordering information on page 186.)

Young Children in Action (Preschool curriculum)
    By Mary Hohmann, Bernard Banet, and David Weikart (1979)
        High/Scope Educational Research Foundation
        High/Scope Press
        600 North River Street
        Ypsilanti, MI 48197

Parent education resources

How to Talk So Kids Will Listen and Listen So Kids Will Talk
    By Adele Faber and Elaine Mazlish   (1980)
        Avon Books
        Box 767
        Dresden, TN 38225

Let's Work It Out
    By Elizabeth Singer and Yvette Zgonc
        New Reader's Press
        Laubach Literacy Action
        1320 Jamesville Avenue
        P.O. Box 131
        Syracuse, NY 13210   (315) 422-9121

Life Skills for Single Parents
        Bureau of Educational Services
        Box 8158, University Station
        University of North Dakota
        Grand Forks, ND 58202-8158   (701) 777-4421

Looking at Life
        Head Start Publication Center
        P.O. Box 26417
        Alexandria, VA 22313-0417

The Nurturing Program for Parents and Children: Birth to Five Years
    By Stephen Bavalek (1988)
        Family Development Resources, Inc.
        3160 Pinebrook Road
        Park City, UT 84060

STEP Series: Parenting Young Children
    By Don Dinkmeyer, Gary McKay and James Dinkmeyer (1989)
        American Guidance Service
        Circle Pines, MN   55014-1796

You're a Better Parent Than You Think! A Guide to Common Sense Parenting
    By R. Guarendi
        Simon and Schuster
        200 Old Tappan Road
        Old Tappan, NJ 07675

Parent-child interaction resources

ERIC Clearinghouse on Reading and Communication Skills
Indiana University/Smith Research Center, Suite 150
2805 East 10th Street
Bloomington, IN 47408-2698 (812) 855-5847

ERIC Family Literacy Center (800) 759-4723
(offers a line of products to help families read together)

Reading is Fundamental (RIF), Inc.
Programs Division
600 Maryland Avenue, SW, Suite 500
Washington, DC 20024   (202) 287-3220

Reading With Children
Literacy Volunteers of America
5795 Widewaters Parkway
Syracuse, NY 13214   (315) 445-8000

Telling Tales: How to produce a book of stories by parents and their children
By Jan Goethel and LVA-CV Family Literacy Staff   (1995)
Chippewa Valley Publishing
400 Eau Claire Street
Eau Claire, WI 54703   (715) 834-0222
(See ordering information on page 186.)

Resources for evaluation and portfolio assessments

An Evaluation Framework for Family Literacy Programs
    By K.E. Ryan (1991)
        (ERIC Document No. ED 331 029)

Family Portfolios: Documenting Change in Parent-Child Relationships
    By R.J. Popp (1992)
        National Center for Family Literacy
        Waterfront Plaza, Suite 200
        325 West Main Street
        Louisville, KY 40202-4251   (502) 584-1133
        (ERIC Document No. ED 342 819)

Learner Portfolios to Support Transitions in Adult Education
    By Jane Braunger, Sylvia Hart-Landsberg, and Stephen Reder
        Paper presented at Transitions: Building Partnerships Between Literacy
        Volunteer and Adult Education Programs (1994 national conference sponsored
            by U.S. Department of Education, Washington, DC).

        Reprints available from: Stephen Reder, Director
                                Literacy, Language, and Communication Program
                                101 SW Main Street, Suite 500
                                Portland, OR 97204   (503) 275-9500

The Mechanics of Success for Families [Report #1]
    (Evaluation tools)
        Illinois Literacy Resource Development Center
        269 West Clark Street
        Champaign, IL 61820 (217) 355-6068

Portfolio Assessment in Adult, Career, and Vocational Education
    Trends and Issues Alerts
    By Susan Imel (1993)
        ERIC Clearinghouse on Adult, Career, and Vocational Education
        Center on Education and Training for Employment
        1900 Kenny Road
        Columbus, OH 43210-1090

Testing and Assessment in Adult Basic Education and English as a Second Language
    Programs.
    By T. G. Sticht (1990)
        San Diego, CA: Applied Behavioral and Cognitive Sciences, Inc.

Resources for English as a Second Language programs

Chapter 1 Technical Assistance Center/Region C
    1979 Lakeside Parkway, Suite 400
    Tucker, GA 30084 (800) 241-3865

Home English Literacy for Parents: An ESL Family Literacy Curriculum
    By Terdy, D. & Berkovitz, L. (1989)
        Adult Learning Resource Center
        1855 Mount Prospect Road
        Des Plaines, IL 60018
        (ERIC Document Reproduction Service No. ED 313 926)

Language and Culture in Conflict: Problem Posing in the ESL Classroom
    By Wallerstein, N.
        Addison-Wesley Publishing Company, 1983

Learner Assessment in Adult ESL Literacy (ERIC Q & A , September 1992)
    By Heidi Spruck Wrigley
        Center for Applied Linguistics (see address below)

Limited English Proficiency (LEP) Parent Involvement Project Modules
    Minnesota Department of Education, Fall, 1991
        Adult Learning Resource Center
        1855 Mount Prospect Road
        Des Plaines, IL 60018

Parenting Curriculum for Language Minority Parents
    By Grace Holt/Sacramento-Stockton Family English Literacy Project (1988)
        California State University/Cross Cultural Resource Center
        580 University Avenue, Suite A
        Sacramento, CA 95825
        (ERIC Doc. Reproduction Service No. ED 318 281)

Parent Involvement and the Education of Limited-English-Proficient Students
    By Simich-Dudgeon, C. (1986)
        ERIC Digest: ERIC Document Reproduction Service No. ED 279 205

For a list of free publications on adult ESL literacy from the National Clearinghouse on
    Literacy Education (NCLE) for Limited-English-Proficient Adults,
        write or call: Center for Applied Linguistics
            1118 22nd Street, NW
            Washington, DC 20037 (202) 429-9292

Possible funding sources

Adult Education and Literacy/ED
400 Maryland Avenue, SW
Washington, DC 20202-7240 (202) 732-2270

Barbara Bush Foundation for Family Literacy
1002 Wisconsin Avenue NW
Washington, DC 20007   (202) 337-6754

Even Start
U.S. Department of Education/OESE
Portals Building, Room 4400
400 Maryland Avenue, SW
Washington, DC 20202-6132   (202) 401-1692

Head Start
Administration for Children and Families, Program Development
Department of Health and Human Services
Washington, DC 20201-0001 (202) 205-8578

Job Opportunities and Basic Skills Training Program
Family Support Administration/JHHS
370 L'Enfant Promendade, SW
Washington, DC 20447   (202) 252-4518

Library Literacy Programs   (Library Services and Construction Act)
Office of Educational Research and Improvement (OERI)/ED
555 New Jersey Avenue, NW
Washington, DC 20206 (202) 357-6315   [Changes pending]

National Coalition of Title 1/Chapter 1
Edmonds School Building
9th and D Streets NE
Washington, DC 20002   (202) 547-9286

National Institute for Literacy
800 Connecticut Avenue NW, Suite 200
Washington, DC 20006   (202) 632-1500

United Way Of America
701 North Fairfax Street
Alexandria, VA 22314-2045   (703) 836-7100

General bibliography

Bibliography

Anderson, R., Hiebert, E., Scott, J., & Wilkinson, I. (1985). *Becoming a nation of readers: The report of the Commission on Reading*. Washington, DC: The National Institute of Education.

Arangua, E., Hayes, B., & Johnson Kretschmann, K. (Eds.). (1993). *Portfolio assessment: An annotated bibliography of selected resources* [Report]. Madison, WI: Madison Area Technical College.

Askov, E. N. (1993). Approaches to assessment in workplace literacy programs: Meeting the needs of all the clients. *Journal of Reading, 36,* 550-554.

Atkins, W. (1994). *An approach to gathering data for planning* [Report]. Eau Claire, WI: Literacy Volunteers of America-Chippewa Valley.

Auerbach, E. R. (1989). Towards a social contextual approach of family literacy. *Harvard Educational Review, 59,* 165-180.

Barbara Bush Foundation for Family Literacy. (1989). *First teachers: A family literacy handbook for parents, policy-makers, and literacy providers.* Washington, DC: Author.

Beverstock, C., & Newman, A. (1991). *Adult literacies: Intersections with elementary and secondary education.* Bloomington, IN: Phi Delta Kappa.

Bracey, G. (1994, January). More on the importance of preschool. *Phi Delta Kappan,* pp. 416-418.

Brizius, J. & Foster, S. (1993). *Generation to generation: Realizing the promise of family literacy.* Ypsilanti, MI: High/Scope.

Cheatam, J., Colvin, R., & Laminack, L. (1993). *Tutor: A collaborative approach to literacy instruction.* Syracuse, NY: Literacy Volunteers of America.

Chall, J. (1990, July). *How people learn or fail to learn to read.* Paper presented at American Newspaper Publishers Association Foundation Literacy Conference, Washington, DC.

Children's Defense Fund. (1994). *The state of America's children.* [Yearbook]. Washington, DC: Author.

Coontz, S. (1995, March). The American family and the nostalgia trap. *Phi Delta Kappan*, pp. K1-K20.

Daisey, P. (1991). Intergenerational literacy programs: Rationale, description, and effectiveness. *Journal of Clinical Child Psychology, 20,* 11-17.

Darling, S. (1989). *The Kenan Trust Family Literacy Project: Preliminary final report.* Unpublished report, Louisville, KY.

de Avila, M., Lednicky, D., & Pruitt, K. (1993). Family literacy: Holistic approaches to family literacy facilitate learning of at-risk families. *Adult Learning, 5,* 15-23.

Doneson, S. (1991). Reading as a second chance: Teen mothers and children's books. *Journal of Reading, 35,* 220-223.

Dorotik, M., & Betzold, M. (1992). Expanding literacy for all. *The Reading Teacher, 45,* 574-578.

DuPrey, A. (1992). *Maintaining the balance: A guide to 50/50 management.* Syracuse, NY: Literacy Volunteers of America.

Edlund, J. K. (1992). Breaking the 'cycle' of illiteracy in America. *Future Choices, 3* (3), 7-29.

Education News. (1994, February). 50/50 program management system training. Wisconsin Board of Vocational, Technical & Adult Education, p. 7.

Epstein, J. L. (1987). Parent involvement: What research says to administrators. *Education and Urban Society, 19,* 119-136.

ERIC Digest. (1989). Teaching adults: Is it different? Digest No. 82, Washington, DC: Clearinghouse on Adult, Career, and Vocational Education.

ERIC Alerts. (1993). Trends and issues: Portfolio assessment in adult, career, and vocational education. Columbus, OH: Center on Education and Training for Employment.

Fingeret, H. (1993, April). *It belongs to me: A guide to portfolio assessment in adult education programs.* Durham, NC: Literacy South.

Forlizzi, L., Carman, P., & Askov, E. (1993). *Project Lifelong Learning: Five strategies for achieving National Education Goal 5.* University Park, PA: Institute for the Study of Adult Literacy, Pennsylvania State University.

Frager, A. (1991). Adult literacy assessment: Existing tools and promising developments. *Journal of Reading, 35,* 256-259.

Freer, E. (1993). <u>Adult literacy volunteers.</u> ERIC Digest No. 132, Washington, DC: Clearinghouse on Adult, Career, and Vocational Education.

Gadsden, V. (1992). *Conceptual issues in family literacy: Toward a framework* [Report]. University Park, PA: National Center for Adult Literacy, Pennsylvania State University.

Goodman, K. (1986). *What's whole in whole language?* Portsmouth, NH: Heinemann.

Goodson, B. D., Swartz, J. P., & Millsap, M. A. (1991 February). *Working with families: Promising programs to help parents support young children's learning* [Report]. Washington, DC: U. S. Department of Education.

Halpern, R. (1990). Poverty and childhood parenting: Toward a framework for intervention. *American Journal of Orthopsychiatry, 60,* 6-18.

Harmen, D. (1987). *Illiteracy: A national dilemma.* New York, NY: Cambridge Book Company.

Hohmann, M., Banet, B., & Weikart, D. (1979). *Young children in action.* Ypsilanti, MI: High/Scope Press.

Holt, D. (Ed.). (1994). *Assessing success in family literacy projects: Alternative approaches to assessment and evaluation.* Prepared by the National Clearinghouse for ESL Literacy Education (ERIC). Washington, DC: Center for Applied Linguistics & McHenry, IL: Delta Systems.

Huerta-Macias, A. (1993, July). <u>Current terms in adult ESL literacy.</u> ERIC Digest, Center for Applied Linguistics. (ERIC No. EDO-LE-93-03).

Illinois Literacy Resource Development Center. (1992). *Fine tuning the mechanics of success for families* [Report 3: Evaluation and Program Development]. Champaign, IL: Author.

Illinois Literacy Resource Development Center. (1992). *Fine tuning the mechanics of success for families* [Report 4: Policy]. Champaign, IL: Author.

Illinois Literacy Resource Development Center. (1990). *The mechanics of success for families: An Illinois family literacy report* [Family Literacy Programs Report #1]. Champaign, IL: Author.

Illinois Literacy Resource Development Center. (1990). *The mechanics of success for families: An Illinois family literacy report* [Evaluation Report #2]. Champaign, IL: Author.

Imel, S. (1993). Portfolio assessment in adult, career, and vocational education. ERIC Trends and Issues Alerts.

Imel, S. (1991). School-to-work transition: Its role in achieving universal literacy. ERIC Digest No. 106. Columbus, OH: Center on Education and Training for Employment.

International Reading Association. (1994). Family literacy: New perspectives, new opportunities. Newark, DE: Author.

Katz, L. (1992). Readiness: Children and their schools. *ERIC Review, 2*, Washington, DC. 2-6.

Keefe, D., & Meyer, V. (1991). Teaching adult new readers the whole language way. *Journal of Reading 35*, 180-183.

Kerka, S. (1991). Family and intergenerational literacy. ERIC Digest No. 111. Columbus, OH: Center on Education and Training for Employment.

Kirsch, I., Jungeblut, A., & Campbell, A. (1992). *Beyond the school doors.* Princeton, NJ: Educational Testing Service.

Kozol, J. (1985). *Illiterate America.* Garden City, NY: Anchor Press/Doubleday.

Kroeker, T,. & Henrichs, M. (1993). *Reaching adult learners with whole language strategies.* Katonah, NY: Richard C. Owen.

Landerholm, E. (1984). Applying principles of adult learning to parent education programs. *Lifelong Learning, 7* (5), 6-9, 27.

Lehman, B. (1993). For our children: A family literacy project for adult basic education classes. Bloomington, IN: Indiana University. (ERIC Document ED359 506).

Lerner, J. (1988). *Learning disabilities: Theories, diagnosis, and teaching strategies.* Boston: Houghton Mifflin.

Lewis, A. (1993, November). The administration's education agenda. *Phi Delta Kappan*, pp. 196-197.

Lewis, A. (1993, December). Making collaboration happen. *Phi Delta Kappan*, pp. 284-285.

Lewis, A. (1993, June). The payoff from a quality preschool. *Phi Delta Kappan*, p. 748.

Literacy Volunteers of America. (1991). *How to add family literacy to your program.* Syracuse, NY: Author

Literacy Volunteers of America. (1989). *Reading with children.* Syracuse, NY: Author.

Loasa, L. (1982). School, occupation, culture and family: The impact of parental schooling on the parent-child relationship. *Journal of Educational Psychology, 74,* 791-827.

Lugg, C., & Boyd, W. (1993, November). Leadership for collaboration: Reducing risk and fostering resilience. *Phi Delta Kappan*, pp. 253-258.

Machmeier, K. (1993). <u>Developing and implementing a broad-based parenting program in family literacy</u> [LVA Conference Workshop handout]. Eau Claire, WI: Literacy Volunteers of America-Chippewa Valley.

Molek, C. (1991). *Together we learn: Family literacy.* Harrisburg, PA: Pennsylvania State Department of Education. (ERIC Document ED342 901).

Morrow, L. M. (Ed.). (1995). *Family literacy: Connections in schools and communities.* New Brunswick, NJ: Rutgers University.

Morrow, L. M., & Paratore, J. (1993). Family literacy: Perspective and practices. *The Reading Teacher, 47,* 194-200.

Morrow, L. M., Tracey, D. H., & Maxwell, C.M. (Eds.). (1995). *A survey of family literacy in the United States.* Newark, DE: International Reading Association.

National Association for the Education of Young Children (1989). *Developmentally appropriate practice in early childhood programs serving toddlers.* Brochure #508. Washington, DC: Author.

National Association for the Education of Young Children. (1986). *Good teaching practices for 4- and 5-year-olds.* Brochure #522. Washington, DC: Author.

National Association for the Education of Young Children. (1989). *Developmentally appropriate practice in early childhood programs serving infants.* Brochure #547. Washington, DC: Author.

National Center for Family Literacy. (1991). *A strengths model for learning in a family literacy program*. Louisville, KY: Author.

National Center for Family Literacy/Project Literacy U.S. (1990, Spring). *A special report on family literacy*. Pittsburgh, PA: PLUS.

National Center for Children in Poverty. (1990). *Five million children: A statistical profile of our poorest young citizens*. New York: School of Public Health, Columbia University.

Newman, A. P., & Beverstock, C. (1990). *Adult literacy: Contexts and challenges*. Newark, DE: International Reading Association.

Nickse, R. S. (1990). Family literacy programs: Ideas for action. *Adult Learning, 1*, 9-13, 18-29.

Nickse, R. S. (1989). *Noises of literacy: An overview of intergenerational and family literacy programs*. Paper commissioned by the U. S. Department of Education. Washington, DC: U. S. Dept. of Education. (ERIC Document Reproduction Service No. ED 308 415).

Nickse, R. S., & Englander, N. (1985). *Administrators' handbook for collaborations for literacy: An intergenerational reading project*. Boston, MA: Trustees of Boston University.

Nickse, R. S., & Paratore, J. R. (1988). *An exploratory study into the effects of an intergenerational approach to literacy: Final report*. Washington, DC: Office of Educational Research and Improvement.

Nuckolls, M. (1991). Expanding students' potential through family literacy. *Educational Leadership, 49*, 45-46.

Office of Vocational and Adult Education. (1992, July). *Model indicators of program quality for adult education programs*. Washington, DC: U. S. Department of Education.

Padak, N., Rasinski, T., & Dawson, B. (1992). Toward effective family literacy programs. *Ohio Reading Teacher, 27*, 5-9.

Project Literacy U. S. (1993, Spring). *Special report on family literacy from Project Literacy U. S.* Pittsburgh, PA: Author.

Ponzetti, J., & Bodine, W. (1993). Family literacy and parent education. *Adult Basic Education, 3*, 106-114.

Poulton, C. (1993). *Family literacy programs: Adult curricula and evaluation.* Unpublished master's project, Weber State University, Ogden, UT.

Powell, D. (1991). *Strengthening parental contributions to school readiness and early school learning.* West Lafayette, IN: Department of Child Development and Family Studies, Purdue University. (ERIC Document Reproduction Service No. ED 340 467).

Purcell-Gates, V. (1993). "I ain't never read my own words before." *Journal of Reading 37,* 210-219.

Quezada, S. (1991, July). The role of libraries in providing services to adults learning English. ERIC Digest No. EDO-LE-91-03. Washington, DC: Applied Center for Linguistics.

Quezada, S., & Nickse, R. (1992). *Community collaborations for family literacy handbook.* Boston, MA: Massachusetts State Board of Educational Research and Improvement.

Ranard, D. (1989). Family literacy: Trends and practices. *In America: Perspectives on Refugee Resettlement, 7,* 1-4. (ERIC No. ED323 574).

Rosow, L. (1991). How schools perpetuate illiteracy. *Educational Leadership, 49,* 41-44.

Santopietro, K., & Peyton, J. (1991, October). Assessing the literacy needs of adult learners of ESL. ERIC Digest No. EDO-LE-91-07. Washington, DC: Applied Center for Linguistics.

Schweinhart, L. J., & Weikart, D. P. (1986). Early childhood development programs: A public investment opportunity. *Educational Leadership, 44,* 4-12.

Schweinhart, L. J., & Weikart, D. P. (1985). Evidence that good early childhood programs work. *Phi Delta Kappan, 66,* pp. 545-51.

Schweinhart, L. J., & Weikart, D. P. (1993). *Significant benefits: The High/ Scope Perry preschool study through age 27.* Ypsilanti, MI: High/Scope Press.

Seaman, A., & Seaman, D. (1994, May). *Evaluation in family literacy: Questions and issues to be addressed.* Presentation at Third National Family Literacy Conference, Louisville, KY.

Smith, Carl B. (1991). Family literacy: The most important literacy. ERIC No. EJ 425 437. Washington, DC: Center for Applied Linguistics.

Snow, C. E., Barnes, W. S., Chandler, J., Goodman, I., & Hemphill, L. (1991). *Unfulfilled expectations: Home and school influences on literacy*. Cambridge, MA: Harvard University Press.

Staryos, M. & Winig, L. (1985). *Collaborations for literacy: Tutor's handbook*. Boston, MA: Boston University Institute for Responsive Education.

Sticht, T. & McDonald, B. (1989). *Making the nation smarter: The intergenerational transfer of cognitive ability*. San Diego, CA: Applied Behavioral and Applied Sciences, Inc.

St. Pierre, R., & Swartz, J. (1993, October). *National evaluation of the Even Start Family Literacy Program*. Second Interim Report from U. S. Dept. of Education: Office of Policy and Planning. Cambridge, MA: Abt Associates, Inc. & Portland, OR: RMC Research Corporation.

Sweeney, T. (1993, November). *Grant writing from A to Z*. Paper presented at United Way of America Education and Literacy Initiative, Washington, DC.

Taylor, D., & Strickland, D. (1989). Learning from families: Implications for educators and policy. From J. Allen & J. Mason (Eds.), *Risk makers, risk takers, risk breakers: Reducing the risk for young literacy learners* , pp. 251-276. Portsmouth, NH: Heinemann.

Taylor, M. (1992, June). <u>The language experience approach and adult learners.</u> ERIC Digest No. EDO-LD-92-01. Washington, DC: Center for Applied Linguistics.

Teale, W., & Sulzby, E. (Eds.). (1986). *Emergent literacy: Writing and reading*. Norwood, NJ: Ablex.

Thurston, P., Clift, R., & Schacht, M. (1993, November). Preparing leaders for change-oriented schools. *Phi Delta Kappan*, pp. 259-265.

United Way of America. (1993, March). *The literacy series: Family literacy* [Report]. Alexandria, VA: Education and Literacy Initiative.

U. S. Department of Education. (1990, July). <u>National goals for education.</u> Washington, DC: Author.

U. S. Department of Education. (1994, May). *Transitions: Building partnerships between literacy volunteer and adult education programs*. Paper presented at national conference, Washington, DC.

U. S. Office of Technology Assessment. (1993, July). *Adult literacy and new technologies*: *Tools for a lifetime*. Washington, DC: Author.

Valeri-Gold, M., Olson, J., & Deming, M. (1992). Portfolios: Collaborative authentic assessment opportunities for college developmental learners. *Journal of Reading, 35,* 298-305.

Van Horn, B. (1992). *Development and evaluation of a model family literacy program.* University Park, PA: Pennsylvania State University, Institute for Study of Adult Literacy.

Wagner, D., & Spratt, J. (1988). Intergenerational literacy: Effects of parental literacy and attitudes on children's reading achievement in Morocco. *Human Development, 31,* 359-369.

Walberg, H., & Marjoribanks, K. (1976). Family environment and cognitive development: Twelve analytic models. *Review of Educational Research, 46,* 527-551.

Weikart, D. P. (1989). Quality preschool programs: A long-term social investment. (ERIC Document No. ED 312 033)

Weinstein-Shr, G. (1989, October). Breaking the linguistic and social isolation of refugee elders. *TESOL Newsletter,* p. 9.

Weinstein-Shr, G. (1992, February). Family and intergenerational literacy in multilingual families. ERIC Q & A. Washington, DC: National Clearinghouse on Literacy Education.

Weiss, H. B. (1988). *Pioneering states: Innovative family support and education programs.* Cambridge, MA: Harvard Family Research Project.

Wiley, T. (1991). Measuring the nation's literacy: Important considerations. ERIC Digest No. EDO-LE-91-04. Washington, DC: Center for Applied Linguistics.

Wrigley, H. (1992, September). Learner assessment in adult ESL literacy. ERIC Q & A, Washington, DC: Center for Applied Linguistics.

Literacy Volunteers of America-Chippewa Valley
emphasizes product development and dissemination.

The following publications are currently available:

- *Put It in Print,* a collaborative effort from specialists in the fields of adult education, creative writing, printing, and product development. This manual assists adult educators and tutors in teaching the writing process to adult students and then publishing the finished works.

- *Celebrate Writing,* a collection of narratives, poems, and essays written by students in the adult literacy program at LVA-CV. This is an excellent companion piece to *Put It in Print.*

- *Telling Tales,* written by Jan Goethel, with contributions from staff and volunteers in the LVA-CV family literacy effort. This manual guides facilitators through a collaborative parent-child writing project. It defines goals, suggests preparatory activities for preschool children and their parents, outlines production of the illustrated storybook, and lists evaluation methods.

- *While I Am Here,* by Mai Holter and Jan Goethel. This captivating cross-cultural biography tells the story of a young Vietnamese woman's search for freedom and self-esteem. It provides realistic insight into the challenges ESL students face as they strive to adapt to American culture.

For information contact:

Literacy Volunteers of America—Chippewa Valley
400 Eau Claire Street
Eau Claire, WI 54701

(715) 834-0222